Help! Help! When Did This Happen?

I can't be 60-years-old!
I just graduated from High School

Shirley Whittington Brinkley

First Edition 2006

First Edition 2006
Copyright © 2006 by Shirley W. Brinkley

Inquiries concerning permission to reproduce
or
Regarding speaking engagements
Should be addressed to:

Shirley Whittington Brinkley
342 Pineview Drive
Mount Airy, North Carolina 27030-5147
sbbrinkley@earthlink.net

Other books Compiled and Published By Shirley W. Brinkley:

1980-1981 _My Inspirational Cookbook_
For Rebekah Sunday School Class, First Baptist Church,
Mount Airy, North Carolina

1999 _Walking With Christ_ Cookbook (Inspirational/Devotional)
For First Baptist Church, Mount Airy, North Carolina

Cover Design by Cara A. Johnston
Graphic Consultation and Cover Creativity by Cara A. Johnston

Printed in the United States of America

ISBN 978-0-9676547-1-3

Catawba Publishing Company
9510 University City Blvd. Suite 103
Charlotte, North Carolina 28213
www.catawbapublishing.com

This book is dedicated first to
My Lord and Father in Heaven
and then to
My knight in shining armor and the love of my life—
My husband, Claude

Help! Help! When Did This Happen?

I can't be 60-years-old!
I just graduated from high school.

Contents

Foreword

Shirley Brinkley walked into my classroom, sat down on the far left end of the first row, and eagerly opened her notebook and her mind in January of 2004. I must admit that her presence intimidated me. She would belly-laugh at this comment, I am sure, because she was beginning her college studies at almost 60-years-old. Surely *she* was the one who felt intimidated, right? Wrong.

As a first-year English instructor at the community college level, I was still a rookie—still getting a feel for what my students needed, what I could give them and what I needed *them* to give in return. Shirley, in a word, meant *work*. I do not mean this in a negative sense; her presence pushed me as a teacher, and, though she always claims that it was I who inspired her, I could also make the argument that it was *she* who inspired me. At the age of 24, teaching someone who is my mother's age scared the daylights out of me. Now, I knew I had some experience under my belt compared to the 18-year-olds. But what could I possibly teach this woman, who had been married for several decades, given birth to three children, become a grandmother and traveled the world? Apparently, more than I could imagine. I taught Shirley strategies for composition, and she taught me about the important *stuff* in life, learned over six decades of loving; laughing; problem-solving; worshiping; traveling; and growing along the way.

Now, all of this wisdom has been compiled into humorous and accessible tales that all women can relate to, regardless of their age or position in life. The fact of the matter is that we all age. How we deal with that process is as unique and complex as our species, but, the moment I read Shirley's manuscript, I knew that she had a gift—a gift for striking a chord, hitting a nerve—that few people have or know how to employ. This is the essence of Shirley Brinkley, the writer. From the first personal narrative that she ever turned in to me until now, I have known that Shirley has an ability to see the human being in herself, to accept the human being in others and, more importantly, to help us to understand and love the humanity within ourselves.

Kennette Lawrence, MA
Surry Community College
Dobson, North Carolina
July 2006

Acknowledgments

I cannot begin to show acknowledgement to anyone before first recognizing my deceased mother, Helen Hursey Johnson Whittington, whom I knew for a short thirty years. She was always my encourager, helping me to believe that I could do anything.

Thank you to my husband, Claude, who has always allowed me to be myself, to pursue my dreams, and for always being by my side through disappointments and joys. I can't imagine accomplishing anything without you.

Love to each of my children for the stories you have created in your own lives that have helped to put together the stories in this book—especially to my precious daughter-in-law, Tara, who is always there for me with encouraging and loving comments, good ears that listen, and broad shoulders for my support. Your sense of humor and positive words never fail me.

Many thanks go to Claude's and my special friends, Rayburn and Evelyn Wright. You are more like a brother and sister to us than neighbors and traveling buddies. You are always there for us. You are a perfect example of what friends should be like: encouraging, showing interest, and always on call. Thanks, Evelyn, for allowing me to share you with my readers. They will come to love you as much as I do.

I cannot write this without thanking Frank Levering and Wanda Urbanska for being my first writing mentors. In January 1988, *I was a young 42-year-old,* and my enthusiasm for writing was sparked while I was enrolled in your evening classes at Surry Community College in Dobson, North Carolina. You were encouragers—never critical of the writings but always making constructive comments to each writer in the class. I continue to be overwhelmed by your talents and many accomplishments. I consider myself privileged to have studied under your guidance and wise teachings.

And, to you, Kennette Lawrence, my precious writing teacher during my return to classes at Surry Community College, *when I was an older 57-year-old,* I owe a great deal. You may be thirty years my junior, and the young are expected to learn from the old, but you have proven that to be a misconception. You are enthusiastic, intelligent, unselfish, caring, and my second writing mentor. Each paper that I wrote for you only encouraged me to want to write more. Thank you for your directions, corrections, suggestions, proofing, and more proofing of all my papers—especially for this book. Commas will always drive me crazy. Thanks for all the grammar help, and *fixes,* and for making the time for me anytime I have needed to call on you for help.

Dianne Griswold, I can't forget you in these acknowledgements. Thanks for being the sister I never had growing up. Without you I wouldn't have had someone to remind me how old I am each birthday. I love you.

A special thanks to Ann L. Vaughn and Martha Morgan for reading—with skilled eyes—and for correcting overlooked errors during your busy schedules and (at times) stressful life situations. Your honest opinions have been welcomed, and your eagerness for this book to become a reality has been another means of encouragement for me. I consider it an honor to be able to call you "friends."

Andrew Callahan, Senior Manager of Catawba Publishing Company, you have been an answer to many prayers. I have no doubts that God directed your company to me. I cannot find words that will describe how much I appreciate you and what you have done to help me get this book completed. You have been kind and tolerant—gently helping and understanding each time that I have sent you additions, deletions, and corrections for the book. May God continue to bless you in your job and career.

Gratitude also goes to each staff member of Catawba Publishing that, in some way, participated in the publication of this book.

Many thanks to so many people who have encouraged me along the way; there are too many to mention. I believe that you know who you are, the paths we've walked together, and the stories we have shared. Please know, too, that without your encouraging words and positive support, this book may not have ever developed.

Help! Help! When Did This Happen?

Introduction

Don't you put this book down just because you are younger or older than 60-years-old. There is a little something in here for all ages. Men, you might even enjoy some parts of it, too.

This is an introduction to aging as seen through the eyes of your author, Shirley W. Brinkley. I have known for years that I was getting older—as each of us do—and each year that my birthday came around, the years were increasing, but I didn't feel any older, and my outward appearance didn't *seem* to change except the constant ins-and-outs of my waistline.

I had turned 20-years-old, 30-years-old, 40-years-old, 50-years-old, and 60-years-old . . . no big deal; this happens to all of us, if we are lucky—blessed. So many years had passed, but it seemed to have happened so quickly.

During the years from my blemish-free, smooth-skin of youth, until the present unfamiliar skin characteristics and features, I would reflect on what had happened in the past, but the past kept getting farther away than I was realizing.

One day, in early 2006, I was driving home to Mount Airy, North Carolina from Winston-Salem with my husband, Claude—*we had just seen Claude's orthopaedic doctor to schedule a second hip replacement*—and as he dozed, I began reflecting on days, weeks, and years since our marriage; our lives together; my childhood; and how it seemed that only a few years ago I had graduated from high school.

As I reflected on bits and pieces of my life from birth until now, I glanced at my hands on the steering wheel and saw not smooth, soft hands without flaws but, wrinkled hands with strange-shaped brown spots—not freckles. I began realizing that time and wear and tear were catching up with me, and my body was exposing old age in an undeniable way.

Wow, I thought. When did all these body changes happen? I only graduated from high school a few years ago. My skin was smooth then—no blemishes—except what puberty doles out to the young. I could breathe without unbuttoning my waistband. I could run for blocks without hesitating and could stay up all night and keep going like an *Energized Bunny*.

Hence, this book came about. It is a reflection of aging—the aging that *attacks* all of us—how a span of time feels so short, yet swiftly slips by with only a slight breeze against the cheek. These are my thoughts and feelings as I jump from event to event in my life and wonder how I could have gotten to where I am in each event; since I *just graduated from high school a few years ago, how could I possibly be 60-years-old?*

I hope there will be enough humor to keep you laughing—at least chuckle a little—as well as to help you reflect on your years as you are growing older and realize how time seemed to leap from your high school years into a decade or more. It is my desire that you enjoy looking back and try to remember some of the things you may have forgotten, either on purpose or just by chance. As you read, I feel you may even say at times, "*I know exactly what you are talking about.*"

Life is worth living, but it is worth more if we are sharing with others. Sharing with you is making the years over 60 worthwhile for me. Take the time to stop, look back, re-see what you may have forgotten, and for goodness sake, enjoy the few minutes you are giving yourself to read and reflect.

I may not be saying anything you haven't already heard, read, or thought. The world is too old for anything original, although everyone wants to be the first with his or her name in lights, but let's be honest; everything is a repeat of everything else. The one thing that is original in this book is me and my life—the funny, the sad, the painful, the disappointing—stories that reflect the lives of many of us.

As you read, hopefully, you will drift with me throughout my life—sometimes jumping from one time period into another and back again—prior to my turning 60-years-old, and the reactions I am having, and then you will be encouraged to think about your own life during similar situations. I encourage you to reminisce about your own childhood, your parenthood, your marriage, your life, and to relive some of your own past events. Consider some things that helped you to grow wiser because of each experience, whether joyful or sorrowful.

And now, sit down, relax, take a deep breath and join me as I . . .

P

A

N

I

C . . .

Help! Help! When Did This Happen?

Chapter 1

Reflections . . . Entering reality . . . the age of "60"

Following are my first thoughts as I begin entering reality . . . the age of "60."

Help! Help! How can this be? I can't be 60-years-old. I just graduated from high school—Needham Broughton High School in Raleigh, North Carolina. What year is this, anyway? What? 2006? No way! I just graduated this year—you know—the year 1963.

Young-un, don't you laugh at me. I *am* in my right mind—which I might add is *not* 60-years-old.

The nerve of that child . . . and speaking of that child, I believe she called me mother. How can that be? I just graduated from high school. That child is at least 40-years-old. Where did she come from?

Well maybe, just maybe, I am a little older. I remember falling in love with a really interesting young man, and I did talk him into marrying me, and somewhere—some time after that—I remember there were three piles of diapers, but that was only a few years ago. I must be about 22 or 23-years-old.

But, if I'm 22 or 23 . . . what the heck happened to that gorgeous body? What in the world is that roll around the middle of me—close to my waist. . . speaking of. . . where is my waist? Oh my, that's me! ! ! But how can this be? I was so sharp looking yesterday. I must be looking into a trick mirror. What a rotten trick to play on anyone. If I find out who is doing this to me, I'll fix them!

W a i t . . . a . . . m i n u t e. This is no trick. That is me. I am "60," but how in the world can a person be "20" one day and the next day be "60?" My goodness, how time flies. . .

• • • • • • •

Who would have ever thought that time would or could have passed so swiftly when we were so young, when we were in our teens, when we were in high school?

• • • • • • •

What have I missed? Have my eyes been closed? Have I been in a coma?

Let me think about this a bit. I remember the graduation; I remember my first job; I remember when the children were babies; and I remember our first home—a rental house down on Willow Street, right here in Mount Airy, North Carolina, with its wooden floors, one bathroom and two tiny, tiny closets.

It had a perfect floor plan for the children. I remember them running, crawling, and playing up and down the long hall that ran down the center of the house; how they would circle round and round for hours through the dining room, kitchen, hall, living room, and back through the dining room—doing the simple things that kept children their young age happy.

I still feel their presence and hear their precious sounds at play. I still feel how I loved those little children. They were so much fun, such a joy. . .

• • • • • • •

The blessings of motherhood are special gifts from God. These blessings should not be taken lightly. Motherhood should be seen as an honor and a privilege. A woman may be able to give birth to a child, but it takes a special woman to be a mother to a child, whether through adoption or conception.

Some women are not given children, but this doesn't mean that God loves them any less. God blesses these women with different gifts—perhaps the gift to serve, to speak kindly, the gift of benevolence. The gift of understanding and tolerance of others, gentleness, love, compassion; the ability to teach or to lead; the wisdom of God's word and the wisdom of where and when to serve, where and when to speak, or when to be quiet; the desire to be used by God.

What gift have you been honored with?

• • • • • • •

We didn't have much money back then, and I remember that our Sunday outings consisted of walks to Eckerd's and down to the Dairy Center. Gosh . . . it seems like just yesterday.

I remember the family that lived across the street and how our little Jackie and their little Todd would yell to—or at—each other from across the street. They needed someone to play with, but . . . but they just didn't play well together, so Gaye and I would just let them enjoy their friendship or lack thereof from a distance.

We lived in the little house, and they lived in the big house.

Our lives were so different, yet our lives were probably so alike. I wonder if Gaye is older. I wonder . . . did things go by as swiftly for her as it has for me? She was really beautiful. I'll bet she is still a *"Perfect 10."* I'll bet she can even still see her toes! Where has everyone gone? Do you suppose her little Todd is around 40, too? How can this be? When did this happen? It seems like just yesterday.

If her little Todd is around 40 . . . then . . . then that means the young-un that called me mother a few minutes ago must be mine! Oh my, where has time gone? Where has my mind gone? Where has my youth gone? How can I be "60?" I only graduated from high school a few years ago.

Let me think for a minute. I remember a birthday party down at the "Y." There were balloons, and a cake, and lots of little boys, and a few little girls. I remember the mothers staying and visiting with one another as the children played games and how they offered to help when it came time to serve the cake and ice cream. The children were so young and the mothers, too. I remember our little Frank—he was called Frankie back then—and some of his friends who came to the party . . . Joey—now called Joseph, Marty, Don, Eric, and . . . oh my, that couldn't have been so long ago, could it?

The phone rings and brings me out of my reverie . . .

Oh, hello Frank. How are things, son? . . . You need me . . . Sure, Dad and I can pick up Baylor tomorrow, we'd love to . . . and Olivia, too . . . sure, that'll be great. Oh . . . Olivia is invited to Andrew's party and Joey will walk her back home after the party . . . You're welcome son, and . . . we love you, too. Let us know if you need anything else, okay?

Back to my thoughts . . .

I'm "60." When did this happen? But it must be! If that was our son Frank and we are to pick up his children, then I am definitely a grandmother. I do know that grandmothers don't come in packages of 20-year-olds. Even "Twinkies" couldn't package a sweetie that good. I just don't know when this happened. Joey, Frank's childhood friend, is a father, too—with a son named Andrew. That must mean that the beautiful young lady, Andrea, is Andrew's mother.

Gosh, how can this be? What went with my life? I can't be "60." I must be under hypnosis! There is no way that I have a daughter in her 40's and a son with two children . . . no way!

Ouch! Well, that pinch did nothing but make a bruise. Wow! What a bruise! I've noticed that since the doctor started me on aspirin that I really bruise easily. Oh my, there comes that thought again. Can it be? Am I really "60?" I'm taking aspirin to help keep my blood from clotting my arteries.   But . . . that's for *old* people, not someone as young as I. I am not "60!" If I'm 60, when did this happen? I only graduated from high school a few years ago . . . didn't I?

Thoughts interrupted with the phone ringing . . .

Hello . . . Well, hello, son. How are you and the girls doing and that precious, sweet wife? . . . Good . . . What's Tara cooking for dinner? . . . mm. . . sounds delicious. Wish we could be there, too. Dad and I are doing fine. Dad is getting ready for his hip replacement. I think he is looking forward to being able to walk like a young man again. (*Oh my, what did I just say—a young   man . . .*) Would you like to talk to Dad? Hug and kiss the girls and Tara for me and tell them I love them. Love you, son . . . here's Dad.

Back to my thoughts . . .

How can this be? Our son, David, has a wife and two daughters. Hayley is 14 and Sheldon is 8 . . . I think . . . maybe 9. David has been in the Air Force for 17 years now. How can this be? When did this happen?

I remember one summer when he and Frank dug a huge hole on the upper lot. I remember that it had rained a day or two later, and after dinner on one of these rainy days the boys must have decided that they had a wonderful swimming pool waiting for them. I guess it didn't occur to them that the water wouldn't be too clean because when Claude and I began looking for them and found them, they looked like two wet, muddy, brown-skinned, unfamiliar boys. The picture of their appearance is still burned in my memory. Once they had enjoyed the rest of the evening splashing and wallowing in the mud-bath-pool, we had them come into the house through the wash room door, only after they were hosed off.

Gosh, that was only a few years ago, wasn't it? Someone is definitely playing a trick on me. I just can't be "60." When did this happen? I thought that getting older took longer than this. I thought it was way out in the future.

Thoughts broken with an interruption . . .

A teenage girl just came in and called me Granny. She looks a lot like Jackie—our daughter—but Jackie calls me mother. Oh, my; this isn't Jackie. It is her daughter, Christina. Christina said her birthday is coming up, and when I asked her how old she would be, she said, "14."

No way! This just can't be. Why didn't someone tell me that just a few years after I graduated from high school that I would be a mother of three grown children and have five grandchildren, and two of the five are teenagers? Teenage grandchildren come to *older* people. Am I *that* old already? Am I really 60-years-old? When did this happen?

I remember that just a few years ago—matter of fact it was October 25th of that year—Claude had to go to Greensboro. I told him that I didn't think he should go because I thought I would be having a baby. I remember that he didn't take me seriously and went on to Greensboro. The next time I saw him, he was visiting me at the hospital. With a laugh in his voice, all he could say was, "*You crazy thing. Nobody is born on Wednesday, October 25th.*" He had always told me that if I wanted him with me when any of our children were born that I would need to have the baby on a weekend when he would be home. When our third child was born, I remember thinking that Claude would be with me because it was a weekend. Thank goodness for weekend babies!

Ah. . . I remember *real cloth diapers*; all the washing, and hanging lines of diapers where the sun and wind would dry them and hoping rain would not come until they were dry. I remember glass baby bottles and formula. I would have the bottles ready for the 2:00 AM feedings. When I heard the baby cry, I would quickly place the bottle in hot water and, while I changed the diaper, the bottle would warm and be ready for the feeding . . .

Seems like only a few years ago that life was so much simpler . . . no complications. Gosh, these births and babies were only a few years ago, weren't they? It doesn't seem like *that* long ago since I graduated from high school. Am I really 60-years-old? . . . How can this be? . . . When did this happen?

• • • • • •

Funny, how we remember things as if it were only yesterday, and how, years later, we still laugh about these things. Have you reflected recently on your child's birth or the birth of a special child of a friend or family member?

Now is a good time to look back and count the blessings of God in the birth of a new life—even if the years that have followed have been difficult. Don't dwell on the painful growing years, but concentrate on the blessings that child was meant to be in your life. Throw out of your mind the heartaches you may have experienced because of that child and draw into your mind the precious moments that he or she gave you—few or many, good or bad—be thankful for what you have had.

Chapter 2

Reflections . . . Reality so very slowly begins to set in

Reflections of life continue, as reality sets in, and I question, how can I possibly be 60-years-old so quickly?

Seems like just a few weeks ago the family was taking an occasional weekend camping trip. The memories are so vivid of me loading the typical *suburban housewife's station wagon* with all the necessary items—the tent (*heavy, thick canvas—unlike the light-weight ones of today*), cooking gear, the top cover and ground cover for the tent to help keep the inside dry, mats for Claude and me, sleeping bags for everyone, stuffed animals for the children, pillows, food, and toilet paper, can't forget that . . . how did I manage to get everything into the back of that station wagon, still have room for the family, and do it all before Claude arrived home at noon from work? Oh my, just thinking about all the *stuff* we needed for those camping trips wears me out now, but back then, I had energy to run on overtime!

Those were the days when . . . seems not so long ago . . . when cash was short—still is—and youth was plentiful. Excitement for the simple things made a camping trip a big event. And, of course, we never left home without our own personal hiking sticks made for each of us by my Claude. Sometimes we had beautiful weather and at other times it was dreary and raining. We learned early in life that the sun was nice, but we could still have fun without the sun.

Gosh, so much time has passed since the children were little. It doesn't seem that long ago, but "60." Am I really 60-years-old? When did this happen? Seems like only a few years ago that I graduated from high school?

• • • • • • •

*Camping for us was like raising our children; we had to learn from scratch what we should do or shouldn't do—what we could not do without and what we could leave behind. The only difference between these two scenarios is that camping comes with wonderful books by "**experts**" with directions and instructions. I now understand why rearing a child doesn't come with instructions and directions. **There are no experts** to write the instructions.*

Each child is blessed with a different personality from the time he or she is born until the time he or she leaves home, gets kicked out, moves back in, moves out again and back in again, finishes college, quits college, decides not to go to college, gets married, gets divorced, listens to our advice, ignores our advice, and on and on . . . How many volumes would a family have room for in their home to cover all the changes? Would there be enough words in each volume to cover the mass of changes for each child, and would a parent have the time to read any of the information?

Thank goodness Claude and I were pretty good at camping—if we made a mistake, no big deal. Unfortunately, we have never mastered parenthood as well as we have camping, but we sure have had an interesting ride (very mildly speaking) as parents, giving parenting our best efforts. Maybe your children and ours will be the **experts** *as they raise their children. Indication is that they are already* **experts***, because most of them don't want grandma and grandpa to have any input, except to baby-sit once in a while.*

Isn't it nice, at times, to be the silent, more experienced, observer? Isn't it nice to know that one day our children will be our age, understanding how we may have thought? Isn't it interesting that they may experience the same anxieties and fears that we have had as their parents? Of course, we'd prefer that our grandchildren would give our children an easier ride and more nights of sleep than some of us have lived through or may still be living through.

• • • • • • •

My friends, please don't look back at all the mistakes you think you may have made while raising your children. As we now know, that is in the past, and we cannot relive anything we did before today. Look at the present. It is here—now—and it is the only thing we can do anything about . . . the now. Remember that we have done the best we **knew** *how to do. Right or wrong, we tried. There is a saying that I use frequently, and I am sure you have heard it before: "It is better to have tried and failed than not to have tried at all." And with that statement I might ask, "What is failure, anyway?" Failure covers a broad scope.*

You have given parenting your best effort. You may feel that you were not a good parent when the children were younger—for reasons only you know—but hopefully, you and I didn't do too much damage. At some point, we must realize that no matter what we have taught, or said, the way the child receives and responds to the teachings is left up to each daughter and son. We have been the potter and no matter how carefully we have added the best ingredients to create a worthy vessel, sometimes it just doesn't adhere and there are cracks and flaws.

Yesterday is gone; tomorrow is almost here. Let your tomorrow be better than today and yesterday. Try to commit to the directions of the Serenity Prayer. Ask God to help you accept the things that you cannot change. You nor I can change a child's lifestyle or attitude. You and I cannot change the past, the present, or the future. Ask God to help you change the things that you can change. Perhaps the change can be within. You and I can change in the way we think—being less critical, staying silent when we want to speak, and showing that we care (without draining the retirement funds dry). Pray that God will help you to recognize the difference—to give you the wisdom you need; the wisdom to know what you can change and what you can not change. (Paraphrased)

• • • • • • •

I remember another time when the children were small, and we decided to go on a picnic after church to Cumberland Knob on the Blue Ridge Parkway.

I remember gathering together the blanket for us to sit on, the bananas, the crackers, the apples, the drinks, the napkins, the plates, and the snacks. I thought about everything that we usually enjoyed on a picnic. I remember . . . oh my goodness . . . I remember, when we got to our picnic site, and I went through the usual routine—spreading the blanket on the ground and placing all the yummies for our lunch on the blanket. Everyone was excited and agreed that it was a great idea to have a picnic. As I was beginning to prepare the peanut-butter and banana sandwiches (I can still feel the shock I had), I realized that I had forgotten the bread. I was so upset, but everyone just laughed and ate peanut-butter and crackers and chased them with bananas, apples and snacks. *Each time we went on a picnic after that, everyone made sure we had the bread, before we left home. I can still hear them ask, "Did you get the bread?"*

Gosh, that was only a few years ago ... wasn't it? I couldn't have been much older than 22 or 23. But how can that be? Seems like just yesterday, and yet. . . I'm "60." When did this happen to me? I know I don't look the same for goodness sakes. I'm no spring chick ... but "60?" You've got to be kidding! Me ..."60"... no way! It seems like I just graduated from high school only a few years ago.

It hasn't been that long since ... since I was a little girl, sneaking to the creek, slipping on the rocks, and getting punished for sneaking to the creek and slipping on the rocks. Gee, that was only a few years ago, wasn't it?

• • • • • • •

What kind of memories do you have of a special, yet simple event that you and your family enjoyed years ago that didn't cost a lot of money? Love filled the moments, and laughter came so easily. Take a moment to dwell on those times and enjoy them all over again. When your days are lonely, try to feel joy and thankfulness for those special times of days gone by. Make a joyful noise unto the Lord that He allowed these times in your life to take place.

You might even try to help someone else make memories. Plan a picnic with a child who needs a grandmother (or grandfather). Show the boy or girl that he or she is special by doing special things with him or her.

• • • • • • •

How long does it take to become 60? Seems like just a few years ago I was taking the children for swimming lessons. I believe they were only six ... or seven ... or eight or nine. That wasn't so long ago . . . was it?

It was just a few years ago that I was coaching girls' softball and was a Brownie and Girl Scout leader. I was substitute teaching at the children's elementary school and junior high.

I just don't understand what has happened with time. I can't be 60. That just hasn't happened yet. I should only be about 20 or 23, yet I know that isn't possible. It seems like I just graduated from high school.

I can remember when the boys were playing little league. Wow, I could really pitch that ball as I practiced with them. I remember practicing with the boys between games; watching them play ball; screaming and yelling for their team; hoping they would make the needed home run for the team to win; and closing my eyes if I thought they might miss a fly ball.

Gosh, seems like that was only a few years ago. How can 60 be here so quickly?

• • • • • •

I hope you have been thinking about some of the many activities you have been involved in since you married and had children—or had children and, for whatever reason, did not marry. Do you remember how there seemed not to be enough time in a day to get everything done before the next activity took place? Not much has changed in past years since we were younger. We still wonder if there will be enough time in the day to get all our activities completed. We are moving a bit slower—at least some of us are.

Then, there are some—for instance, Oprah Winfrey—who will not slow down when they reach 60, or 70, or . . . Oprah will just keep looking better and better and going and going. She must be put together with a little of the glue that created the familiar Energizer Bunny.

Chapter 3

Reflections . . . Piecing the years together

Reflections continue as I try to piece the years together and understand how I could be 60-years-old so quickly. . .

As I finish putting away the clean laundry, my mind begins to wander back in time, and I'm thinking . . .

These clothes are only mine and Claude's. Why is this? I only have to match Claude's socks. Where are the boys' socks? . . . Where are Jackie's dresses with the cute pinafores? All I wash and iron these days are Claude's dress shirts for church and a few of my things. Seems only a few days ago there was more laundry. I don't understand.

Are the children doing their own laundry now? Can this be? It hasn't been so long ago that I had them collecting the hangers from their closets for my next batch of laundry, reminding them that if they didn't put their dirty clothes in the hamper or the laundry room that I would not wash their clothes. My goodness, what a liar I became! Once in a while, I would be tough, but usually I would give in—they needed clean clothes, even if the dirty ones didn't land in the hamper. Putting their dirty clothes in the hamper didn't predestine whether they would be responsible adults or not. The children turned out favorably in spite of me, not because of me.

Seems like only a few years ago that the children were taught to make up their bed when they got out of it, before they came down for breakfast. I remember, not so long ago, that I would have juice and milk with bacon and eggs, or waffles, or pancakes, or some type of hot breakfast on the table for them before they went to school and how they were allowed cold cereal only on Saturdays.

Saturday breakfast for our children is now an everyday breakfast for today's child. Homemade waffles and pancakes are now from the grocery freezer and filled with preservatives. Milk was whole milk back then and now many of us are drinking skim milk—not a bad move health-wise, but it sure is hard to adjust to seeing through the milk to see the cereal before the spoon finds it.

It wasn't so long ago, was it, when the children were in kindergarten? I remember the time when David fell from the—seems like 20-foot slide, and Claude was called to pick him up and bring him home. David had left his show-n-tell—which happened to be his constant companion—and Claude had to make a return trip to the kindergarten classroom to pick it up. I can still feel the fear in my heart, praying that David had not gotten hurt seriously from the fall. I remember watching him so very carefully for the longest time. That couldn't have been too long ago, could it? It seems like only a few years ago ... but I am "60," aren't I? How can this be? The fall must have happened at least three decades ago.

Sure doesn't seem that long. How can this be? Seems like only a few years ago that I graduated from high school. I just can't be "60," can I?

I can remember . . . oh my . . . the first trip we took with the children to Disney World. Gosh, that was only a few years ago . . . I think. I can feel the excitement the children had. My goodness . . . seems like just yesterday—the ride down on an Amtrak Train—our first train trip. The children stayed up all night going from car to car. I remember that a child from another family dared David to swallow a dime. I was so frightened. I just knew he would choke to death . . . seems like only yesterday. Jackie, Frank and David just laughed at my fear and reminded me that what went in the mouth would come out the other end—eventually.

And then . . . our trip back home. The funny things we do to bring home a little of our vacation. We made a special trip to a road-side stand to purchase "*Florida Oranges*," and purchase oranges we did. We finally made it to the train after driving in torrential rain, on the flat highways of Florida in a rented "Gremlin" (*an American Motors compact hatchback*), and stalling numerous times because the car sat so low to the road that the water would drown out the engine.

Wet, but in our seats, laughing and thankful that we made it before the *"All aboard"* signal, we began enjoying our "*Florida Oranges*." As we were really getting into the peel and the sweet fruit of the oranges, Claude, in his wisdom, made a brilliant (*sarcastic*) statement, "Wouldn't it be funny if the oranges are not from Florida?" I remember looking at him and telling him that would not be funny at all. I didn't even want to think about the oranges not being from Florida after what we had gone through to get them. Claude looked at the location where the oranges were from. I remember how disappointed the children and I were when we learned the oranges were not grown in Florida, but that didn't stop us from enjoying our **California** oranges all the way home.

• • • • • • •

I hope you will take a few minutes to think about the fun you and your family had on your first big trip that was planned just for the children. Look deeply and remember everything you can about each event. It'll be fun to think about, and the joy will last for a while. You might even take the time to call the children and tell them you think they are special and that you love them; even if you do it every time you talk with them, once more isn't too much. Is it?

• • • • • • •

The trip to Disney World doesn't seem so long ago. But it must have been. Disney World was celebrating its 5th Anniversary, and I can remember, only a few years ago, it was celebrating its 25th Anniversary or was it the 30th? or 35th? So easy to forget how long ago and yet to think everything happened in such a short time.

Maybe if I pinch myself, I will shock myself back from the nightmare I am having. Nope, I know I don't need another bruise, but if there is one thing that I do know . . . *I know that "I AM NOT 60!!"* I can't be! It's not possible! I just graduated from high school a few years ago.

Let me think about this a bit. Let me do a little math. Now, I was born in 1945 (that's a fact) . . . and if this is really 2006 (that is also a fact) . . . and if I subtract 1945 from 2006 . . . then I am . . . . "**60**." Let me do that again. 2006 − 1945 = "**60**." How can this be? Okay, try this another way. 2006 − 60 = 1945 . . . the year I was born. I just can't believe this. "**60**!" **I'm "60!"** It just can't be this way. When did this happen? I know it hasn't been so long ago since I graduated from high school.

Only a few years ago, I was playing Hide and Seek with the children. I could hide in "*small places*" and not get stuck because of my body size. When I got down, I could get back up—on my own. It hasn't been *that* long since I was helping the children with their homework.

Just a few years ago, I could balance myself while standing on my hands or while doing cartwheels. Now, the only way I can stand on my hands is if I place them under my shoes and step on them. Now, the cartwheels I can do are in my head, in my imagination, where I am safe, and my arms don't bend at the elbows before I have gotten into the hands-on-the-ground position.

I remember, how, just a few years ago, I could move the furniture from one side of a room to another side of the room, *all by myself*. Why is it that now, I can't do any of this? Is it that I am getting a *little* older? Sure, a little maybe, but "**60**"? No way. I only graduated from high school a few years ago.

● ● ● ● ● ● ●

Now is such a good time to think back to when you were able to do so many things that you may not be able to do now. Stop. Take a look back. Think about the energy you had and the many foolish things you would do, never realizing there could be any danger in the games you played or the many different activities you were involved in during your youth. Wasn't youth fun? If you can't recall some fun things you did as a child, maybe you're not really concentrating. Sometimes, these fun things were in our imagination.

Perhaps you had a rotten childhood, with uncaring or abusive parents. Don't begrudge what you didn't have, but be thankful that you have lived until today. None of us can return to one second that has passed, but we sure can advance into the second that is to come—God willing.

Hopefully, you have tried to become a person that is better than your circumstances as a child. God allows each of us a second, and third, and many more chances to become someone better than we were. It is never too late to improve. I believe that our circumstances, whether good or bad, provide the map that determines our lives. The roads we take from those circumstances are our decision. Age doesn't determine our destiny unless we allow it to. Make changes now for yourself or help someone else to make changes.

Become a part of a young person's life that may or may not be related to you. Help that young person have good things happen in his or her life. Use your imagination. It doesn't cost dollars and cents to be kind and give a little of yourself. It only cost your time. You may have heard that before; now prove it to be true. There are many doors you can open that will change another's life, for the best, whether he or she is young or old.

Give up self and become a giver. What I call the "me syndrome" needs to be done away with. No one wants to hear, "I . . . I . . . I . . ., Me . . . Me . . . Me." Learn to place others before self. Age becomes less your constant thought and more an avenue to grow and to help others grow. (Hello, Shirley, are you listening to yourself?) Our communities and churches have many opportunities for us to volunteer. Helping with delivering meals-on-wheels to the shut-ins, visiting nursing homes and taking time to really visit, helping in Women's Shelters or being the driver for someone who needs a lift to the grocery store or doctor's office are a few of the many opportunities just waiting for you.

Chapter 4

Reflections . . . The "Twilight Zone" . . . Scars, reunions, loss of a friend

Time passes, and here I am again . . . thinking . . .

What are these scars on each of my shoulders? What in the world has happened to me? Looks like I've been in a fight with a switch-blade knife. I haven't, have I? Oh my, surely not rotator cuff repair? On both arms! This can't be. That happens to *'old'* people, or heavy machine operators, or sports people. *I'm not 'old'*. I'm not a heavy machine worker. I'm not a sports person. What is going on here? When did this happen? How can this be? I'm not *that* old! I can't be "60". I know I only graduated from high school a few years ago . . . I think I know.

There has got to be a clever explanation for what is happening to me. I must be traveling through a terrible, crazy, time warp, and I can't find the door to get out. I know . . . I'm in a "Twilight Zone." Well, I surely can't tell some of my family members that or they will tell me that I've been living in a Twilight Zone for years . . . What's new?

Okay, where am I . . . Who am I . . . How old am I?

Why you crazy woman, you're right here. You haven't moved, but the way you are thinking, it could be that your brain has taken a serious vacation!

I just don't understand how this can happen. Only a few years ago . . . let me think . . . Only a few years ago I was born, then I grew, then I went to elementary school, then high school, then I got married, and then I had three children. Now . . . somewhere between the children and now, only a few years have passed, and I am suddenly 60-years-old. I just don't understand how this can be. I closed my eyes shortly after graduating from high school, and then I opened my eyes, and suddenly I am 60-years-old. It just doesn't happen that fast . . . does it? Well, guess what Granny-Babe? I think it has.

I wonder if this ever happens to anyone else. This is crazy. I'm young one day and old the next. I don't remember it happening that way with people I've known—my grandmother, for instance. She was always old. I don't think she was ever a teenager. My mother is another person that . . . well, let me think about that a minute. . . No, I can't remember her ever being young one day and a few days later being 60. I don't even remember her being 60. She was suddenly 65, and then she died. Gosh, I never thought about it before, but her life moved rather quickly, and then it was over. How can this be? Isn't living supposed to take more time before one dies?

What have I missed during these *few* years since I graduated? I don't think I've missed anything. Everything happened rather systematically and was at times chaotic. I went to bed—woke up—cooked breakfast—took the children to school—cleaned house—prepared dinner—read books—enjoyed sports—made friends—worshiped—loved—cried and laughed. Nope, can't think of a thing I've missed, yet, the interesting thing is that all this was supposed to have taken place in 60 years of my life. How can this be? I remember the day I graduated from high school, and that was only a few years ago.

This reminds me of the song that has the words: . . .*close your eyes, turn around, and you're a young girl* . . . This is the way all this feels to me—I have closed my eyes, turned around, and I am out of high school; closed my eyes, turned around, and I am married; closed my eyes, turned around, and I am a mother of three; closed my eyes turned around, and I am a grandmother of five; closed my eyes, turned around, and here I am—"60." I've decided that I don't like closing my eyes and turning around. Life is passing too quickly, and I just can't be "60." How can this be? When did this happen? I know that I graduated from high school just a few years ago.

Time passes, and thoughts begin to swirl again . . .

Seems like a few years ago I went to my fifth class reunion, and then the next one was the . . . What? . . . This is the WHAT? . . . This can't be the 40th class reunion . . . No way! How can this be? We only graduated a few years ago!

Good grief, look at these classmates. Some of the ones I remember the most look older than they did a *few years ago.* Surely, I don't look *that* way, too? Are they as shocked as I am?

Well, some things haven't changed. Some of them are still drinking more than they should. Some of them are still the same snobs—still captive to their arrogance. The cliques are still very much alive and well. Those that ran together in high school are dining together tonight and bring each other up to date on the past years of their lives. Those that think that they have "*made it*" are telling it, and those that are content with where they are simply listen.

Not a lot has changed since high school. There are big towns and small towns; large neighborhoods and small; wealthy people and poor still have cliques of friends, just as it was in high school. There are still arrogant people, and there are still some very humble people. There are sad and lonely people, as well . . . Life goes on.

I'll bet some in the class came just to see what every one looks like and to show everyone how good they look. Wow, some actually do look pretty good—must have had a face lift, belly tuck, or had that *Botox* 'stuff' injected under their skin to fool the wrinkles into thinking they aren't there. I'll get a little closer to see if I can see any needle marks . . . Oops . . . not a good idea. Oh well, the rest of the crowd looks like they are at least 60-years-old. Mercy me. . . . This just can't be—we're all at least "60"—where has the time gone? Seems like just a few years ago we graduated from high school.

I can remember when I could stay up all night and part of the next day, and I never seemed to tire. I could dance and dance until the floors were rolled up. Now, I roll up before the floors are warm with the dancers. Bedtime feels so good at 9:00 and sometimes even 8:00 in the evening.

"Sixty" . . . How can this be? ? ? ?

• • • • • • •

What were your thoughts at your last class reunion? Be honest, now. What did you do to prepare—lose weight, get a tummy tuck, spend too much money on new clothes? Did you put on a false impression, or were you the person your true friends know today?

*Have you changed much since graduation—physically, spiritually, intellectually? Were you "**the arrogant snob**" in high school? Have you become an arrogant snob since you graduated? Has your placement in life created a monster or a ministry? Has your love for acquiring worldly things—stuff—occupied your thinking and directed your lifestyle? Have you become wiser—more knowledgeable of what truly makes a person happy?*

High school years were exciting and a good experience for some of us, but for others of us, they were painful and tough. The best part of high school is that it was a part of our lives that vaulted each one of us into the real world. Who we were in high school did not predestine our future. That was up to us and the direction we took out of high school. Have the dreams you had back then been reached, or did God give you a new direction?

At age 60—or at any age—we should still be learning. We are not there yet! We should be reaching for the stars as we did in our youth, but those stars should be heaven bound. Joyce Meyer has said, "Just because you don't believe there is a Hell, it doesn't mean that you can't go there."

• • • • • • •

As I reflect on my school years and those of my classmates that did not live to participate in their first, fifth, or thirtieth class reunion, I give thanks to God that I have been allowed to live to be 60-years-old. My mind takes me back to Hugh Morison Junior High School (long since replaced with a Federal Postal Distribution Center) and a beautiful classmate that I remember and can see as clearly as if she were right here in front of me . . . Linda Tisdale . . .

I was immediately struck by her natural beauty. Linda was the most beautiful girl that I have ever seen or known. She had just moved to Raleigh from up north, and we became friends quickly in our ninth grade classes; it's easy to become friends with someone when you are constantly telling her how beautiful she is, as I so often did to Linda.

Linda wore make-up, and I didn't, mainly because I did not know how to put it on without looking like I used a Maybelline Starter Kit without directions. Hard as I tried, even after Linda so graciously taught me how to put on make-up, my make-up never did for me what Linda's did for her.

Her skin was beautiful . . . without a flaw. Her lips were perfectly lined and the lipstick applied carefully and skillfully. Her brows were perfectly arched —the shade of a soft, mellow, brown with hints of red—like an artist carefully sketches a woman's brow on paper with a terra cotta pencil. Linda was a real, live, porcelain doll, with beautiful, smooth, and flawless, cream-colored skin.

Seems like such a short time ago we were classmates, and then we graduated. Linda married either just before we graduated or just after graduation, and then came . . . her terrible, terrible, unbelievable death . . . She was gone . . . The terrible pain of her sudden absence left her young husband, her mom, dad, and brother to struggle with her absence and no doubt to question why. They would never know the joy of holding the precious baby she was carrying—to watch it grow, hear it laugh, watch it play. The aneurism or hemorrhage gave little warning . . . She was gone.

• • • • • • •

The impact of Linda's death touched many lives, as does the death of any young mother, or wife, or child, or parent, or husband. Linda left me with so many good thoughts of her—of how she unselfishly gave of herself to be kind to me, something I was not often familiar with from other classmates. Linda touched my life in a way that has traveled with me until this day. I don't put make-up on that I don't subconsciously say thank you to Linda. At times I'd like to say, "Linda, thank you for making the effort to teach me the skills of applying make-up correctly. I sure wish you were still here to give me refresher classes."

My friends, there may be someone who left an impression in your life. Don't hesitate to let that person know. Don't wait too long. Your expression of appreciation to that person could make a difference to him or her.

Linda was a perfect example that there is always someone watching us. We should strive to be the best that we can be at all times. No matter what our age may be, our actions will always be observed by others. Our actions and words can influence someone in the wrong way or the right way. When given the opportunity, I tell young children, pre-teens, and teens that someone is always watching them; therefore, it is important to set a good example.

Each one of us is a mentor to someone, even at your age, whether you are 60-years-old or 20-years-old. Are you setting a good example for that someone who may be watching you?

Chapter 5

Reflections . . . Too much stuff . . . Too much dust . . . You can be replaced

As I was entering the dusting and cleaning mode one day, these thoughts began invading my mind . . .

Well, I've put this off long enough. If I don't get started, another day will go by, and the dust will be a little *deeper*. I can't believe I'd rather stay home and tidy up the house than shop. Shopping just doesn't have the meaning it had when I was younger. I have **all** the **stuff** *that I thought I needed* to make me happy . . . Can this be? Enough stuff? When did this happen? Where did all this stuff come from?. . . Why am I hanging on to all this stuff?

Dusting takes so long anymore. I have too much stuff, and everything has to be moved from one spot to another to do a thorough cleaning—too many little things; too much big stuff; too much furniture; too many rooms. Why didn't I listen to my mother-in-law years ago when she told me that I had all that I needed—and I thought I didn't have anything? She told me that, the more stuff you have, the more stuff you have to move to dust. Why couldn't I have learned from her and followed her wise advice? Acquiring things comes with a price, besides the price in the money spent purchasing the things. It's a shame that youth has to age in order to become wiser.

Seems like only a few years ago we moved into our new, CLEAN, home, built just the way we wanted it. The house had lots of room to move around in, very little to no furniture in some rooms—so much space and nearly no stuff—how simple life was then . . . How much easier and quickly I could clean.

I remember the third-me-down furniture; my mother-in-law's, then my sister-in-law's, then my mother-in-law's again, and then we got what was left of it. The five of us had to sit three to the couch and one in each chair. If that became too soft, or we just wanted a different place to sit, we would resort to the floor. No big deal; we were more agile back then.

We all watched the one television that we owned, and there was no discussion as to which channel. We could choose between one of three channels or choose to do something else altogether.

• • • • • • •

Take a look back in time to your earlier years, to your first home, and to the few items it took to accomplish a daily cycle of living—just a few pots and pans, just enough dishes for each family member, just enough money to make it from paycheck to paycheck. Some things may not have changed for some of us. Some of us may still be living from paycheck to paycheck. Could this be because we bought too much stuff along the way? Now, we may be thinking, "Do I really need this item or that item?"

Now may be a good time for a yard sale, which, I might add, I utterly despise. I have had two yard sales in my lifetime, and after the last one, I decided that when I die, if I end up in a yard sale, I didn't go to heaven; I ended up in hell.

If yard sales are not your thing, then the next method of getting rid of some or all of the stuff is through donations. Give to a needy family or families; give to the Salvation Army or Goodwill; or perhaps Habitat for Humanity could use some items, but be considerate. Don't give away useless items. Be sure that what you give away is useable. Too many pots and pans you've accumulated over time can now be handed over to someone with zero to few. It's easier now to determine what we can do without than it will be later on when a change in our lives may dictate a move to a smaller home, the home of a child, a rest home, or retirement facility.

One good way to remove items that you thought you couldn't do without is to place small items in a box as if you were going to put them in storage. Set the box aside for awhile—several weeks or a few months. Once the items are out of sight, thus out of mind, you probably won't miss them, so get rid of them.

Young people, there is one thing that you will learn as you grow older; no matter how much you have in material items, none of it will be enough to make you happy. Take a serious look at people you know who keep buying and buying. You can see that they have all they need. Are they really happy? Don't get into the same life of materialism and wish later that you had been more frugal. The money has been spent, the items have accumulated, the dusting must be done, and the 'stuff' must be moved.

• • • • • • •

As I continue cleaning, I begin thinking . . . remembering . . . when the children were young and Claude was traveling (as usual), I al-

ways tried to do the housework so that when he returned home, I could spend my time with him.

Dusting has never been a favorite past-time, and I have always put that job off as long as I could. In order to encourage me to do the dusting, Claude always made that job interesting for me . . .

Now as I dust, I remember how. . .

Claude would date the dust when he found it. Sometimes, I found it with a really recent date, and sometimes I would let the dusting go until I was *lucky* enough to see a date deep in it. *I remember how* . . . Claude would find places that needed dusting and would place money close to it, or inside something that I had to move in order to dust. Wow, the extra spending money I could have had if I had only dusted more often.

I remember . . . I always had a bad habit of leaving the up-right vacuum cleaner in the upstairs hall rather than putting it away. I always had the intention of using it again before I put it away, but, my friend, procrastination took over. I remember . . . once, I had left the vacuum cleaner in the upstairs hall a little longer than Claude must have thought I should have. Each time I would pass by it, I would think . . .

I either need to vacuum or to put the cleaner away, *but, as time had a way of taking care of things, there sat the cleaner when Claude came in from another trip. He asked me one evening as I was preparing dinner*, "When did you vacuum?" Puzzled, I remember asking what he meant. He told me that a week or so back, he had placed a $20 bill under the cleaner, and he just looked and saw that it was gone. He wanted to make sure I found the money and had not vacuumed it into the cleaner. About the time he was telling the story about the money, David (*our youngest son*) was passing through the kitchen. David said, "I found the money, Daddy."

Claude was relieved that the money had not been wasted into the vacuum cleaner, but I was a bit miffed that I had not found it. I told David he owed me that money because it was left for me. I didn't get all the $20; David split it with me. Shame on me; that money was rightfully David's. Guess I need to make things right and give David the other $10. I remember the conversation like it was only a few days ago . . . but how can that be? David has been living away from home nearly eighteen years.

Such a short time ago, it seems, I graduated from high school. Surely, I'm not "60", am I? I was only "50" a few years ago. Three-fourths of a year have passed since I turned 60, but it seems like only a month or two. How can this happen so fast?

• • • • • • •

Can you think of something humorous that has taken place during your cleaning? Think hard. Surely cleaning hasn't always been hum-drum.

Did you spend too much time making sure the house was in order and not enough time playing with the children, or the hubby, or becoming a friend with others? I heard a story many years ago of the lady who was always so busy keeping her house clean that she didn't have time to visit with friends, and when she got old, she had no friends. I hope this is not the story you have to tell.

For those of my readers who are still young, may I urge you to take a look at your priorities? The house will keep. There will always be dust and dirty floors. If you are married, make your life now with your husband. The children will someday move away and have a life of their own; therefore, if you neglect your spouse while the children are young, what will you have left of your marriage when the children move out?

Take time to pamper and adore your man. Men, take time to

pamper and adore your wife. Let that person know how special he or she is. Ladies, get your house work done while the children are asleep, or playing, or in school, and the husband is at work. Be ready for your man when he arrives home. If you don't give him the attention he needs from you, there are other places and people that will fill your void. This happens every day.

If you are a mother working outside the home, a gold crown you surely deserve. You really have to be imaginative, creative, and organized to juggle the time needed for your husband. But that special time alone with your man is essential for him and for you. It's well worth the effort, so don't feel guilty that you have left the children with yet another sitter or there are things in the house yet undone. Value one another, and show it.

I heard as I was growing up that cleanliness is next to godliness. I believe that going overboard trying to keep everything spotless can also keep us from God. We're too busy to pray. If we are cleaning all the time, we don't have time for a quiet time with the Lord—quality quiet time. We don't have quality time for our families and fun time with our family and friends. Dear friend, be so very careful that which you place as your priorities.

• • • • • • •

The previous comment, "If you don't give him the attention he needs from you, there are other places and people that will do your job for you," reminds me of my wedding day.

I remember that special Saturday, June 11th at 2:00, standing in the pastor's study—just me, Claude, the pastor and our immediate families. I was thinking . . . Today is finally here. I will be getting my two-year degree—my   M-R-S Degree . . . My Mrs. Claude F. Brinkley Title.

How I had worked to get to this point. I had begged Claude to marry me for so long that he was finally going to, just to get me off his back. This is the story I like to tell when young girls or older women tell about their romantic engagement and how they were proposed to. My engagement and proposal doesn't sound real, but it's not too far from the truth.

I remember the moment the pastor pronounced Claude and me husband and wife. Just before the sealing kiss, Claude whispered in my ear the words that are still ringing, "I love you, Shirley . . . and, don't forget, *you can* be replaced." I remember, and can still hear, the chuckle he gave after those words. Then, we both laughed.

This remained our secret . . . perhaps the family wondered what Claude said to me and what we were laughing at, but that was for only us to know . . . our secret. Those words left an impact with me throughout our marriage, and I have tried really hard "not to be re-placed." I was wise enough to know, even back then, that Claude's words were said for a little humor in the ceremony, but I took them seriously.

Marriages are meant to have humor. Everything that is said between a husband and a wife doesn't have to be all seriousness. We must learn to laugh with each other and allow ourselves to be laughed at, without taking it personally. Always pamper, love, adore, serve, admire, and compliment one another. Who wants to replace a spouse that does all that?

I am reminded, too, of another statement Claude made to me several years after our wedding day.

As a young wife and mother—with tremendous insecurities—I would constantly tell Claude that I loved him. And, like so many young women, I wanted to hear, "I love you, too, honey." Claude would respond occasionally with "I love you, too," or "I love you too, honey," but I never heard it as much as I needed to. Finally, one day, in one of my hormonal states, I asked him point-blank. "Claude, do you love me?" He said, "Of course I do; why?" After my emotional explanation, he assured me that he loved me with these words, "I married you, didn't I?" Then came, "On our wedding day, I told you that I loved you, and if I change my mind, I'll let you know."

Well, that took care of that. He's still here. I'm still with him here, and the neatest thing has happened. He now tells me all the time that he loves me and without me prompting him.

Girls—ladies, if you will—take the time to wait and see what happens in your marriage. Just because he doesn't tell you all the time that he loves you doesn't mean that he has stopped. He may have the same thoughts that Claude had. He will let you know if he changes his mind.

Chapter 6

Reflections . . . Suddenly liver spots . . . Depends . . . Doctors' visits and such

Reflections as I experience physical changes that appears to have happened suddenly . . .

Well, good morning, legs. Who crawled in bed with you last night and drew those strange purple roads all over you? Some roads are heading to various provinces of Canada, some to St. Louis, some to Boston, and others lead to Florida, Texas, California, and Washington State. They just start nowhere and move in all directions.

Land sakes, what has happened to my freckles? I still see a few, but what in the world are those strange-looking brown spots that seem to be splattered all over my body? I didn't have them yesterday. They just came. I went to bed with freckles and woke up with these disproportionate spots. They are everywhere. Oh my, do I have a terrible skin condition? I know what I'll do; I'll walk up to Evelyn's and let her take a look at them. She's a retired nurse and will know real quick what is going on . . .

After making a frantic call to my friend and telling her that I needed her to take a look at something for me, I enter her home with . . .

Well, here it is Evelyn. What do you think? . . . Why are you laughing? . . . This is serious! Evelyn, a best friend doesn't laugh when her friend has a problem . . . What? These are what? These "gosh-offal," ugly brown spots are . . . *liver spots*. Evelyn, how can you laugh at such a terrible condition? I didn't even know I had a liver problem. Are these the symptoms I'm going to have as my liver progresses from bad enough to much worse? Will these spots grow together and make me look like I have developed a natural tan? Is a natural tan the only good that will come from this terrible condition?

"No, No," she said, "Those spots have nothing to do with your liver. People get those spots when they get older." Older . . . Oh my gosh; she said it. My friend said that I am old. How can this be? I can't be old. When did this happen? I can't be "60" . . . I just graduated from high school a few years ago, didn't I?

Once I regained my composure and regained my footing, Evelyn and I began to laugh at my thoughts, and I said to her . . .

"You know, Evelyn, I'm a little relieved—not that I was delighted to learn that I could have had a liver problem—but the idea of the spots growing together and giving me a nice tan wasn't such a bad idea."

• • • • • • •

Can you handle the truth from a friend? How do you react when others tell you the truth or point out things about you that you'd rather they ignore? Are you a gracious receiver of what you are being told, or do you lash out? Take a moment and think about the laughter you would have missed in life if God had not sent you a special friend to call on at any time. We all have God, who is on call at all times. He loves us just as we are, brown spots and all, and so do the friends that God sends our way.

• • • • • •

Sometimes, visits to the doctor can cause strange reactions . . .

What is happening to me? I feel just fine, except for a little dizziness once in a while. Why has my doctor decided I need to take Gemfibrozil for my cholesterol and Benicar HCT for my blood pressure? Most people start taking this kind of medicine when they are many years out of high school—when they are "old." It hasn't been so long ago since I graduated. I just don't understand, and now he is telling me that my dizziness is nothing to worry about . . . it's only benign positional vertigo. He didn't even bother to tell me which position I should avoid and what the vertigo had to do with my dizziness. Let me think . . . benign . . . malignant . . . which one gets worse? I am so confused.

What is happening to me? I can't be old. I can't be "60". I think I am a clear thinker. I think I understand what I am told. I think I am confused. I think I *am not* old. I think I'd better not think. Maybe I do need a doctor—I think.

• • • • • •

Another visit with the doctor—this time for a physical. . .

I can't be "60." Just the other day, I went to the doctor's office for my annual physical. The doctor greeted me with, "Hello, young lady. How are you these days?" After the examination, the doctor told me that everything looked good, except that I would need a bladder tack because my bladder was falling out.

What? How can this be? *I am thinking* . . . What in the world causes a bladder to fall out? *With this thought* . . . I asked him, and I cannot believe what he said. He said it was because of my age and having children. What kind of nut does he take me to be? Didn't he call me *young lady* when he saw me at the beginning of the visit?

I know, and I know that others know; there is no way I could have aged that quickly—young one minute and old the next. Impossible! Right? . . . Right! I told him there was no way I could be old enough to have a bladder falling out of my body; I only graduated from high school a few years ago.

He looked at me like he might consider committing me to a place with four guarded walls, and then, slowly, very slowly, but precisely said, "How can that be? Your records show your birthday to be in 1945 . . . that makes you 60-years-old."

Confused . . . I am! Old, I am not! I'll show him. I tried to spring off the examination table but realized the spring had rusted, and all I could do was ask for a hand getting off the table so I wouldn't fall and break a bone.

Once I was dressed and the doctor returned to the room, he asked if I was incontinent. "In what continent?" I asked. I live on the North American continent. Are you crazy, doc? I'm thinking to myself.

I just don't know what gets into some of these intelligent people's heads sometimes. He had my address as Mount Airy, North Carolina. Didn't he know Mount Airy is on the map, in the United States of America? Couldn't he be smart enough to know that? And he thought my bladder was falling out. What does he know?

He then said that he would try asking the question another way. "Do you need Depends?" he asked.

I responded, "Depends . . . depends on what?" He tried to explain that it depends on my falling-out bladder—or something like that. I know I'm not the smartest critter, but by golly miss molly, I do know if my bladder is falling out; I know that I live on the North American

Continent, and I know that doesn't *depend* on anything unless I move out of the United States and way north, or south, or east, or west.

Before I left his office, he asked if I was having any dizzy spells. What a question. I wasn't having any dizzy spells until I came for this examination—now my head is spinning around with all this stuff I'm hearing that doesn't make a bit of sense to me. I thought going to the doctor would do me a world of good, but I must say—I'll follow my mother's advice from years ago—don't go to the doctor unless you are sick.

After the visit with the doctor . . .

What an experience. I am worn out. I guess I need to go by the cafeteria for lunch, relax and shake the doctor's visit from my mind . . .

Oh, my. There sure are a lot of *old* people that eat here. I heard someone say that the initials for the C & W Cafeteria stood for canes and walkers. My goodness, do you suppose? It appears that I am the youngest one here. I feel out of place.

How can this be? I'm moving as slowly as the rest of the people. I'm drinking decaffeinated coffee . . . just like they are. I'm getting cornbread and pintos . . . just like they are. I sure like my piece of coconut custard pie . . . just like some of them do. What's going on here? I need someone to carry my tray for me . . . just like a few of them are doing.

This just can't be! I'm too young. I just graduated from high school a few years ago. I can't be "60". The doctor just can't be right about my age. Shame on him for saying it—shame on me for believing he's right.

• • • • • • •

Is it a bit tough to accept that, physically, changes are taking place, and your body isn't quite what it was when you were younger? I never realized that my body would take so many different direc-

tions in health and appearance. I thought that when I was younger, it wouldn't bother me if I got wrinkles—I was not that vain, but you know what? I have to admit it—I am bothered. I don't know if I have been so influenced by the media, magazines, and articles that throw appearance, appearance, appearance at me, but my appearance does make a difference to me. I guess my appearance has always been important to me, but not to the extreme that it is to some.

How do you react within when you see someone your age or older who is physically unable to feed themselves or is struggling to walk or speak because of a stroke? What reactions do you deal with within yourself when you see someone your age, or older, who is carrying an oxygen tank with him or her wherever he or she goes?

Certainly, it bothers you. Certainly, it is normal to wonder if this will happen to you. Life is getting shorter and shorter. The comment I heard once—that we begin to die the day we are born—is more real to me now. Life is shorter. Birth is so far in the past and death is nearer—whether we want to admit it or not. One of my granddaughters says that I am so morbid. Well, facts are facts, and there is no point in denying the inevitable. Really, what are our options? We live, we die; life goes on or life ends.

Geoffrey Chaucer—considered the greatest poet of the middle ages—is credited with the phrase, "Time and tide wait for no man." Those words had no meaning to me until now, at age 60. Time has passed and hasn't waited. One blink of an eye, and that moment is gone forever. I find it interesting that this was said by a man who lived to be 60, or thereabouts (1340? – 1400).

By-the-way, I wasn't throwing off on the C & W Cafeteria, better known around here as K & W Cafeteria. It is a good place for anyone to have a meal. Older and younger people tend to eat the wrong foods when eating alone, and the cafeterias tend to prepare a good variety of foods for everyone's tastes. I'm glad to have them around.

When I run out of ideas for what to prepare at home, one visit to the cafeteria, and I have rejuvenated my meal planning.

• • • • • • •

Once, I had two good eyes, and now I am known to myself as four-eyes. I now wear glasses. This creates more thoughts about aging . . .

These glasses are driving me crazy. When did I get these things, anyway? What is happening to me? It hasn't been long since I graduated from high school, and I wasn't wearing glasses then. These have those strange lines near the bottom of the lens. Bifocals! That's crazy . . . bifocals are for much older people.

I remember, sometime in the past few years, that I wore half-glasses. Let's face it, sugar; they were *Granny glasses—what I call old-lady glasses—t*he type the librarian always wore in high school with the chain hanging off of them. I became her, chain and all, except I wasn't a librarian. I used them for reading only. Why keep them *slung* over my nose all the time if I wasn't reading something?

But these bifocals have recently arrived to torment me. Recently; did I say recently? Let me think about this a second. I started wearing the Granny glasses when I was 40 . . . FORTY . . . when did that happen?

I graduated from high school when I was 17. Somewhere between 17 and when I started wearing glasses, something must have happened. I don't remember sleeping for a long time, because if I had, I wouldn't be so tired.

Oh, my . . . another time warp. Scottie . . . PLEASE beam me up!

I must have started wearing these things very recently. I have fallen so many times, trying to see through these things, that I feel like a drunk that doesn't believe he is drunk. I guess the next glasses I get will be *trifocals*. For me, the top will be for driving—to see great distances; the middle will be to use at the computer; and the bottom will be for reading anything other than the computer. (*I understand* that there really are trifocal glasses. One section corrects distance, another section corrects medium vision, and the third section corrects near vision. . Shucks, I thought I came up with an original).

This is ridiculous. I just don't understand when all of this has taken place. Did my eyes decide to stop letting me see clearly one day and just take a vacation? One day, I had better than 20/20 vision, and now I have astigmatism.

Everything is *sneaking* up on me—young one day and old the next. Seventeen-years-old one day, and then "I'm 60". It hasn't been that long since I graduated from high school. I'm not really "60" . . . am I? It has happened too quickly.

• • • • • • •

Changes do come as we get older. Some changes we can do something about, such as our weight and keeping our cholesterol and blood pressure in check; but some changes we have to learn to accept, such as wearing glasses, or contacts, the birth of liver spots, or those rough flat "warts" that just seem to spring up everywhere that the liver spots haven't already landed.

Are you grateful that you can still see, even with the help of glasses? We can at least close our eyes if there are things we'd rather not look at.

My mother was blind in one eye and had terrible vision in the opposite eye. She would always tell me to donate my eyes when I die so that someone else could see. This has been my plan for many years, but I learned several years ago that I have a degenerative eye disease—Macular Drusen. If the vessels in the eyes were to rupture, and the macular were to float up to the center of the vision of sight, I would be limited as to what I could see. This could happen, or I could live the rest of my life without a problem; so, wearing glasses is a blessing, and I am so thankful my sight is as good as it is.

Count each blessing you have—each and every one; you never know when your health could take a different direction. Don't be a whiner; be a praiser.

Chapter 7

Reflections . . . Childhood and cookies and a very special teacher

Time passes, and as I am looking through some picture albums, reflections of years gone by are beginning again.

For goodness sakes, when in the world were those pictures taken? Oh my . . . Look at the date on them . . . Sakes alive; that's me back in 1971. Gosh, that was the year we moved into the same home we are in right now. Oh my, that was a l·o·n·g t·i·m·e ago . . . . . Watch your mouth, Mama! You're stepping on delicate ground talking like that.

Look at those trees. They were nothing but twigs when we moved here. What happened to them? Did we cut them down? Nope. I don't remember it if we did. They are now huge. How can this be? I didn't see them grow that tall. Wasn't I living here while they were growing? Is this what is happening to me? Have I changed that much, too?

Oh my; here's a picture of me one Christmas with the children. We were baking Gingerbread Cookies . . . That's me! You've got to be kidding! I sure don't look like I did in 1971, or '63 when I graduated, but how can this be? When did I change? Does time really move by so swiftly?

I remember . . . not so long ago . . . when I was eleven or maybe twelve, and I could twist a boy's arm and his whole body would flip. Doesn't seem possible, but I can see it happening just like yesterday. Now, why in the world would I remember something so ridiculous? . . .

I remember catching Crawdads down at the creek. (*We, the neighborhood children, called them Crawfish.*) I remember when my grandma and I would play Rummy, and she would always get mad at me if *she* didn't win. I can remember, like it was yesterday, going with mother to work at the Minute-Grill Truck Stop on old Highway Number 1 North, where she was a waitress. I remember sleeping in the booths, in the section that was closed for the night, until mother would get off work. I still hear the music being played from the selections made by the truckers on the small juke boxes at each booth. That wasn't so long ago—was it? Seems as though I just graduated from high school only a few years ago . . . can I really be "60?"

I can remember other times when I would walk to the State Capitol Building on Sundays, when mother would be working at the Carolina Hotel as a dishwasher, and the fun that I had climbing all over the statues. No one is allowed to do that anymore. Some political person, or statue protector, or some type of *expert,* has made the decision that if the statues are climbed on, they will be damaged, or deteriorate, or self-destruct, or something. What a shame; the simple fun children of today are missing that I got to enjoy as a child. I sure can't imagine how sitting on the saddles of horses that are statues could hurt anything. Oh, well; life still goes on.

• • • • • • •

What are some of the things you can remember doing as a child

. . . your memories . . . that children today will never be able to do? What are some of the things your children made memories doing, that their children are unable to do today? Maybe it's time you jotted down your childhood activities for your children to know about. Remember that "time and tide wait for no man," but know that words on paper can last forever . . . Sorry, time warp – words on a DVD will also last forever . . . I think.

• • • • • • •

I remember when Mother and I rented our house out and moved into an apartment across the street from the state capitol in downtown Raleigh. That apartment building is gone now to make way for more modern, more *important* buildings. I remember so well, mother telling me to always close the door to the apartment so the pigeons would not go in, and I remember . . . oh, how I remember, the day I left the door open *on purpose*, just to see if the pigeons would really go inside. Oh, my . . . seems like just yesterday that a pigeon did go through that opened door and up a flight of stairs into our apartment. Seems like just yesterday that Mother was upset with me for not obeying her, but she loved me anyway, forgave me, and never mentioned it again—except for a good laugh.

Was that so long ago? How can I be "60?" It hasn't been that long since I graduated from high school . . . has it?

• • • • • • •

Time continues to swell many memories into my mind . . .

I remember having to ride the city bus to Hugh Morison Junior High School and each afternoon walking by the bakery near the city bus stop. Mother and I had so little extra money (*Daddy, out of the goodness of his heart, sent $7.50 a month when he felt guilty or the law caught up with him*), but somehow I would manage to save a little lunch money so that, once a week, I had enough money to buy me a big, soft, sugar cookie at the bakery, near the bus stop that was across from the state capitol.

I can still feel the wonderful soft texture of those big cookies as I would bite into them. The flavor is still imbedded in my memory. I quietly enjoy in my mind how I would bite slowly into them and so completely savor even the crumbs. I guess those cookies are why I love baking soft sugar cookies to this day. I never bake cookies that I don't think about those incredible, big sugar cookies. Seems like just yesterday . . . but how can this be. I just can't be "60," can I? When did this happen?

• • • • • • •

Some of our childhood memories are extraordinary, and we never want to forget them, and then there are some memories that we are left with that are painful, and we are still scarred from them. This thought, of being scarred, caused me to reflect on an event that took place in junior high school . . .

I remember . . . oh, how I remember my junior high school home economics class and of the time that each student had to make an outfit. I was so excited. Mother and I picked out the most beautiful material I had ever seen—at least it was beautiful until I made my outfit. I don't believe that I'll ever forget. I begged the teacher to not make me model my outfit in front of the whole school. It was so ugly—big, yellow flowers on a deep blue background. I can still see it. I had made a one-piece jumper that, when I put it on, made me look like—like, I can't begin to describe how I thought it made me look.

The teacher made me model it, along with each of the other students. I was the last student to cross the stage, and the entire student body roared with laughter. I was so humiliated. I can still hear the laughing. I cried all the way home that day. I didn't even ride the bus—I walked. I still feel the hurt and humiliation of that day—a moment in time that has been my tag-a-long.

Seems like just yesterday—the piercing pain from the laughter—but how can that be? I now have grown children of my own. I have grandchildren. My Claude and I have been married so many wonderful years. I just can't be 60 . . . can I? I only graduated from high school a few years ago . . . didn't I?

. . . and then I remember a wonderful teacher that made a positive difference in my life . . .

I remember vividly when I was in the third grade, at Emma Conn Elementary School—just a block down the street from where I lived—and when I was chosen to be the *"Queen of Hearts"* by Miss Calhoun. How could that have happened to me? I had never before or since gotten chosen to do anything special in school. I remember Miss Calhoun telling the class that she had picked the person that she thought would make the best Queen. I still can't believe she chose me.

Miss Calhoun was the kindest teacher I ever had in school, and she always told me that I could do anything that I wanted to do, if I would just try. I learned that year, from Miss Calhoun, what it was like to be loved by someone other than my mother. The third grade has remained my favorite grade in school, and it seems not so long ago, almost like yesterday.

I remember . . . gosh, how could I ever forget? School for that year was ending, and Miss Calhoun talked to me about how she thought I should spend my summer. I don't remember her exact words, but I remember her telling me, "Shirley, I want you to practice your writing this summer; and I want you to read your summer "Weekly Reader" every day; and I know that when school starts back and you are in the 4th grade, you will be the best reader in the whole class; and you will have the prettiest handwriting of all the girls in the fourth grade." She told me that she wanted me to go to the city library, and get me a library card, and that she wanted me to read, read, read all summer.

Oh, how I loved Miss Calhoun. I remember how mother had to work hard to pay the twenty-five cents a week for each Weekly Reader; but I promised Miss Calhoun that I would try real hard during the summer; and I promised mother that I would read every one of those Weekly Readers, if she could just let me get them. I wanted Miss Calhoun to be proud of me, and my mother had taught me that, when a person makes a promise, the promise should be kept.

I remember that I kept my promise. I remember that I couldn't wait for the mail to come each week, because I would have mail addressed just to me. I remember . . . I remember practicing my writing over and over again. I remember watching the changes in the letters as I tried and tried to write better and better.

I remember the long, hot, summer walks to the city library—that was near the capitol (*just a wee bit over three and a half miles round trip and quite a walk for a third grader loaded down with books*)—every two weeks to check out books to read. I read, and read, and read all summer, and when school started back, and I visited Miss Calhoun to let her see how my writing had changed, and I read to her . . . I remember how proud she was of me. I still hear the excitement in her voice, and I can still feel the big hug she gave me, and I can still hear her say, "Shirley, I knew you could do it. You're a smart little girl."

Miss Calhoun made a real difference in my life. I wish there were more teachers like her.

I know the third grade was a long time ago, and when we are in the third grade, it seems like forever and ever before we will graduate, if we even think about it at all. Once we graduate, life goes by so swiftly, yet, I remember the third grade and Miss Calhoun, as if it were only a few years ago. Am I really "60?" It doesn't seem possible; it wasn't so long ago since I graduated.

• • • • • • •

*Teachers are the professionals that can motivate or destroy a child's ego and self-esteem, either by their actions toward a child, or not listening to the anguish in a child's voice, or not reading the pain in a child's eyes when speaking to the child with a wrong tone of voice. Children are human beings with **real feelings**. All children need to be encouraged and made to realize that they are special, no matter who their parents are, or where they live, or the kind of clothes they wear, or the color of their skin or nationality. Children are loaned to the teacher—as they are loaned to the parents, for a short time, and the love shown to that child may determine the direction that child will go in life. If you are a teacher—or a parent—what impression do you leave? What kind of memories will your students, or your child, have of you?*

Being a teacher today is a stressful and, oftentimes, a thankless job. Being a teacher, a good teacher, one who doesn't burn out in a few years, is a job that few are able to master. It's tough to smile and think positively each and every day, nine months of the year, for 20 plus years. I pray for each teacher that is faced with a class of young people that are hard to reach, and I ask that anyone reading this will lift these teachers up in your prayers. The teachers need constant help from our Father in Heaven to be a mentor for each child, and your prayers and mine can make a difference to each teacher and to each student.

Chapter 8

Reflections . . . From Goldie Hawn to old age stinks

On the cover of a recent AARP Magazine, there was a picture that stirred my thinking again about age and appearance . . .

Well, hello missy. What are you doing on the cover of a magazine for senior citizens? You aren't there yet, and it will be a while longer before you are.

No way; Goldie Hawn isn't 60-years-old. Well, maybe she is and the cover editor pulled an old picture from the files of when she was 30-years-old. There is no way anyone can look like *that* and be 60-years-old.

Well, actually, the male species manages to look pretty good as he ages and most of the time looks younger than his age. Look at our present President George W. Bush and former President Bill Clinton. They both will become 60-years-old this year. Republican or Democrat, it doesn't matter. Men just look good naturally—no make-up, just a clean shave and neatly trimmed and combed hair. (*You decide which one you prefer. I have my pick, and I'm not telling which one it is.*)

Just a few days ago, I complimented someone I hadn't seen around town for years on how good she looked, and she responded with a gracious, "Thank you. I can thank my mother for that. It was in the 'jeans.'"

If 'jeans' have anything to do with looking good, then I want a pair of brand name *jeans* exactly like the ones that Goldie wears.

I remember that . . . I didn't start wearing jeans until Frank and David were playing ball, and jeans were the right attire for a ballgame. Maybe, if I had started wearing them earlier in my life . . . maybe, just maybe . . . they would have squeezed the ugly out of me and squeezed some *purty* back in.

I love wearing jeans now, but I hate the first day I try to put them on after they have been washed. I can't even zip them up.

I'm thinking . . . if I needed to describe how to put on a pair of jeans, I would explain it this way, so beginners listen up . . .

The process is to first put your socks on and pull them up—before the jeans go on—not a pretty picture—so be sure your bedroom door is locked. Theory behind putting socks on first: if the jeans go on first, you will not be able to bend over and reach your feet until the jeans have stretched to fit the shape of the lower half of the body; therefore, socks go first.

The next step is to pull the jeans up, and prepare the mind to convince the lower half of the body that it is not lady-like to leave the zipper down. Now, in order to zip the jeans into a completely closed position, and then button the waistband together, you will need to place your entire body in a supine position on the bed, so the belly (the abdomen, for those of you who are anatomically intelligent) will fall toward the backbone and the struggle is less intense.

Once you stand, breathing comes in half breaths until the brain realizes that this is the most oxygen it will be allowed and until the waistband realizes and concedes to the thought that, "this crazy lady thinks I am three inches thinner than I am."

Once the jeans are up, zipped, and buttoned, I make sure there is little that I have to do that will require bending until the waistband has reached the full proportion of my physical waist, and oxygen has reached its full potential for the brain to function as normally as possible by a "60-year-old" granny in jeans.

Warning: Keep in mind that once the jeans are up, zipped, and buttoned, you may experience excessive heartburn and, because of the lack of oxygen to the brain, there may be dizziness and strange behavior. Prepare friends and family the day your clean or new jeans go on so they will be conscious of your actions and strange facial expressions.

After time has passed and the jeans have taken the shape of my body, **they feel wonderful**. I put off washing them as long as I can, or until I have the energy to go through the process of remolding them. Buying larger jeans would be an answer to the torture, but then I couldn't say I wear a size 16; but then, what difference does it make anyway, since I respond the way I do when someone asks, "What 'cha up to, Shirley?" Without hesitation, or regret, I respond with, "174 pounds (or whatever I weigh), as of this morning . . . thanks for asking." Realistically, most people can look at me and can see that I'm not a size 9. I wore a size 9 diaper when I was born, and I've been increasing in size ever since.

• • • • • • •

Speaking of clothes and how to put them on brings back memories of an incident that happened and the way I handled it . . .

I remember, so clearly, while the children were in school one warm, spring day, and I had to make a visit to the grocery store. Once I had taken the children to school, I decided to swing by the store for my regular grocery adventure. I had worn a favorite, yellow, knee-length short outfit, with an elastic waist and large pockets that were open from the side to easily slip the hands into.

As I entered the store, and proceeded to place my car keys into one of the pockets, I ran into a major road-block of a problem. There were no pockets. Where did they take off to? How could this be? When I put my pants on, they had pockets, and now the pockets were gone. Strange . . . I remember glancing down to see if I had put on what I thought I had. Then it hit me . . . I had put my pants on backwards.

What would any sane, young lady do at this point? Why, any sane, young lady would go home immediately and return another day, with her pants on the correct way, right?

Not me; no siree. My sanity has always been a bit questionable to some close relatives and a few friends. I remember that, rather than leave the store, I went over to the produce section, got close enough that I could see my shorts in the slanted mirror above the produce, and attempted to diagnose my situation. Standing in an awkward position, like models walk—throwing their lower torso and legs about a foot ahead of the rest of their body—I began to slide my hands into my pockets that, once in place, lay conveniently over my hind-end. I did this several times—for what reason I cannot explain—and then I decided that my shirt would cover my hind-end enough so that no one would know that I had my pants on backwards.

Fortunately, the pants were clean, and my belly filled the spot the hind-end was now filling, and the hind-end was filling the spot that the belly would normally fill. No problem.

Well, I could have made it through the store, gathering all

that was on my list, and no one, except me and God, would have known that my britches were on backwards; but, as I passed a friend in the first aisle after the produce section, and we exchanged pleasantries, I had to tell what I had done—mouth of the south, big mouth Brinkley, tell it all mama—that's me.

A friend, whose name is Kathy, asked how I was doing. I responded that I was fine, except that I had trouble putting my britches on the right way before I left home. Kathy thought that my inability to dress correctly was so funny that I heard her laugh at different intervals throughout the store. As I would see her at different locations, she made a point to tell me that she was so glad she had seen me, because I had made her day. Well, honey, just call me "Miss Clint Eastwood." Let me make your day.

• • • • • •

Imagine that; my carelessness in dressing became a blessing to someone else. Can you think of anything, that didn't start out to be what it was supposed to be, that turned into a blessing? Can you laugh at your mistakes and share with others, so they can be blessed and realize that you are as human as anyone?

Have you ever worn two different shoes to work, or somewhere, and when you realized it, you wanted to hide until time to leave? I realized one day that I had worn mismatched shoes, and rather than letting it ruin my day, I just let those around me know that at home I had another pair just like the ones I had on. Everyone got a good laugh, and the atmosphere for the day was anything other than stressful.

Have you ever been walking, and because you didn't raise your feet high enough, you tripped? Rather than look around to see who may have seen you trip, you may as well keep walking; it will be less obvious. You know . . . and those around know . . . that you tripped, and you know, there was nothing that caused you to trip, except your rubber sole shoes, or your lazy feet.

Pride sure can mess up a good 'trip'.

• • • • • • •

Walking past the mirror early this morning jolted me a bit . . .

Oh my . . . this just can't be . . . there's someone in the mirror looking back at me . . . Who are you, old woman? Where did you come from? Where is me? . . . Don't you stand there and mock me . . . Shame on you for doing it, and shame on me for letting you do it to me.

There you go laughing, but how can this be? The sound of your voice sounds just like me. I am so young—at least 22 or 23—and you are so old, so how can this be? Look at those wrinkles; there's no hair on your brows, your lashes are missing, and you're so short and round. Your hair looks awful. Your skin is so old, and the hairs on our legs are just about gone.

No . . . no . . . this cannot be. That person I'm looking at . . . just can't be me. That person is old . . . not as young as I am . . . I can't be "60." When did this happen to me? I graduated from high school in '63. What did you say? This is 2006 . . . Can't be . . . Can it? It hasn't been that long since I graduated from high school.

I have been noticing some changes, but it seems like everything happened at once. Suddenly, I seem so much shorter. I used to be able to reach things that I now need a step ladder for. Could it be true . . . that I have shrunk? Oh yes, my sweets, you are an inch and a half shorter according to the last physical . . . remember?

Well, no wonder I'm shorter; I'm bigger in the middle. The *shrink* squeezed me from head to toe and made me more round. What a sight to see. Where, for goodness sakes, did I go?????

Another sighting . . .

Okay, I give up . . . What in the world is that below my chin? Where did that come from . . . that funny looking *stuff* dangling there? I don't remember it being there when I graduated, or when I married, or after the birth of the children. Where did it come from? How can I describe it? Well . . . let me think . . . It looks like a blob behind my chin, and parts of it looks like I borrowed some of the turkey's neck before he was harvested for our Thanksgiving meal. I think I will call Evelyn. Maybe she will know . . .

Evelyn—in her gentle way—defined this blob as a double chin, and that *wrinkly stuff* did not come from the turkey's neck. As she gently explained my strange body changes, her words trailed off into sort of a chuckle; then, round, and round, we went again about age, me not being a spring chick, but "60" . . . How can this be? Sixty or not, we're still friends. . . I'm sure we must be; why else would I allow someone to be so *honest* with me?

• • • • • • •

More thoughts are floating in my head, as my age continues to torment me . . . or . . . as I, at some point, face reality of what my age is . . . "60" . . . and it is not holding there . . .

Help! I don't like any of this stuff that is happening to me. Getting old wasn't supposed to happen so quickly. It was to happen much later in my life.

I hear people speak of senior years as the 'Golden Years'. What is g**old**en about being **old**? Gold is supposed to be valuable, but what is valuable about being closer to your death than the day you were born—other than the assurance that you will spend eternity in Heaven? Sixty is over the hill, and the only direction from the top of the hill is down, down, down, . . . except when I go up, up, up to Heaven . . . but then I'm dead, dead, dead.

Golden = **G** I'm **OLD**; the **en**d.

I went to Wal-Mart the other day—you know, the store that is like a river with many tributaries—it is branching out everywhere. As usual, as I went through the automatic gliding doors, I was greeted by a senior citizen, and I thought . . .

Well, it'll be a while before I qualify for that job, but it sure is nice that Wal-Mart thinks about *that* age group. I'm just too young right now—there are lots of years before I am eligible for *that* position . . .

But how can that be? Just this morning, Claude and I ate at the Waffle House, and we made a point—as we always do when we eat away from home—to order from the senior citizens section of the menu. Maybe this is the golden part of the "Golden Years." We save about two Golden Sacagawea Silver Dollars for every two waffles we order with coffee. Let me think . . . the theory behind that is: spend $6.41 to save $2.00 . . .

This, my friend, is the senior mind in action . . . sounds a bit like the young ladies that shop and spend $60 to save $20 on a new pair of shoes. There has to be some logic in that somewhere. Wouldn't it be more frugal to not spend any money and eat at home? That way, we would still have those Golden Sacagawea Silver Dollars mixed in with the $6.41 plus tax.

People say that old is only in a person's mind . . . yeah, right. That's easy for a 20 or 30-year-old to say. Old is not 20, or 30, or 40, or 50. It's 60, or 70, or 80, or 90, or forever. If old is in the mind of the person, why do so many changes take place in the body of an old person that do not take place in the body of a young person?

For example: I recently saw a young lady—in her very early 20's—bend at the waist; brush her hair down toward her knees; raise back up quickly and fix her hair; and continue on with her activities—without missing a beat.

There is no way I could ever do that . . . at my age . . . because if I attempted to bend over and raise back up as quickly as she did I would be laid out on the unfriendly, cold—thank you for catching me—floor, in less than a split second after raising my head back up—if my head even made it back up.

• • • • • • •

Reality punctures holes into my innermost being, as I contrast being old versus once being young . . .

When I graduated from high school, I had energy to spare; I never ached; I could see clearly; I would hear everything. My teeth were strong (*sounds like someone purchasing a good work horse*), and they didn't crack or break so easily. My hormones were produced by natural body reproduction, and now, a little purple or blue pill is my means of hormones. This is not youth, my friends . . . this is old age.

The monthly ritual has been gone for years—probably the best part of aging. My ovaries are the size of a pea; my gallbladder is non-existent, and my bladder has a mind of its own. When I want to sleep, it wants to go; when I want to walk, it wants to run; when I feel the need to fill up on liquids, it feels the need to empty. This is old age, and it's not in my mind . . . it's running out my bladder and soon down my legs.

There is no point in living in a state of denial. Old age stinks, and anyone that tries to convince me that these are the best years of my life is usually a much younger person, who still has all her body parts—that work without the help of medications or fruit and fiber for regularity. The only thing that is the same as when I was young is that I still get out of bed in the morning with bad breath, wild looking hair, and sometimes even gas.

No matter how well I take care of myself, progressively, unpleasant body changes are taking place. No matter how young I *think* I am, the mirror doesn't lie. A few years ago, I could see a firm body—wrinkle free—and today my top laps onto my middle, and my middle laps onto the top of my legs. My arms were strong when I was young, and today, I have what my son, David, calls a *fish belly* that dangles from my arm between my arm pit and my elbow.

How can this be? I looked like me yesterday, and today I look like my grandmother. I don't like any of this that is happening to me. Getting old wasn't supposed to happen until later—much, much later in life—at a very slow pace, so I could be introduced to me in my latter years in a careful and kind way. All of this is just slapping me in the face—with power punches, bruises, and ugly, obnoxious, *liver spots.*

I will not look in the mirror! . . . Not one more time. I will not believe that the person I used to be is gone. I don't remember a funeral or packing up and leaving. I am still right here . . . in the same skin; it doesn't look like much, but it is mine. I do not remember a skin transplant or lypo-filling. That's right *old* girl, a lypo-filling. You have more fat . . . not less, so you couldn't have had a lypo-suction.

Perhaps . . . the reason I don't remember any of this is because . . . I really am . . . "**6 0**". . . I grew out of my 20-year-old skin and grew into my 60-year-old skin when I wasn't looking.

I'm really not "60" . . . am I? Didn't I just graduate from high school a few years ago?

Chapter 9

Reflections . . . That'll never happen to me

We can never tell when something unusual might happen; when our sight and hearing begin to fail us . . . as we get OLDER . . . our hair takes its own direction . . . our mind wanders, and wanders, and wanders, and . . .

As I am out for an afternoon drive, my thoughts turn to how things have changed since I first got my driver's license . . . not so long ago . . .

I sure don't see as well as I did a few years ago, and my reflexes aren't quite as quick as they used to be, either. Guess it would be a good idea to drive a little slower.

For goodness sakes, what is that driver behind me blowing his horn for? Oh my; the light just turned red . . . When was it green? . . . Thank goodness that light finally changed . . . I can see in my mirror the irritation of the driver behind me.

Well, there he goes, trying to race me to the next light. I guess he likes to hurry up and wait, since I am now beside him, and now, we can *speed* off together when the light changes.

And then . . .

Drivers sure are impatient these days . . .

Land sakes . . . I turned before the light was red. Sounds like an orchestra of horns behind me. A dog must have run out in front of those cars; surely they are not blowing at me . . . Why would I even think of such a thing?

Oh my . . . blue lights—looks like the officer wants to talk to me . . . I can't imagine why. I'll bet it's my nephew . . . wanting to show me his children's pictures . . . I sure wish he would turn off those blue lights before he gets out of his patrol car.

Hello, officer . . . why, you're not my nephew. . . I did what? . . . Didn't I hear the train?. . . What train? No sir, I didn't see the train, nor the flashing red lights . . . Yes sir, I heard a horn, but I thought people were blowing at a dog in the road . . . Yes sir, I sure do wear glasses, but I only wear them when I need to read something. You know, sir, they make me look so much older than I really am. It hasn't been so long ago since I graduated from high school.

What's that, officer? Would you mind speaking a little louder? . . . Do I wear hearing aids? . . . Oh, I sure do officer, and I wouldn't be without them. There is so much noise pollution that I keep them turned down so I can think.

Did you say that you think I need to turn them up? . . . I could have been run over by the train? What train, sir? I didn't see a train, and I certainly didn't hear one.

Now, now . . . Don't try to scare me. I know you are trying to do your job, but don't you think it would be a good idea to let the engineer know that he needs to blow his horn a little louder for those *old* people who have trouble hearing?

Thank you, officer, for warning me about the dangers of not

keeping my hearing aids turned up and not wearing my glasses .
. . I will try to be more careful, sir.

Oh, my . . . no, sir . . . I don't need an escort home. I only live a few blocks from here, and the blue lights would scare the neighbors to death, not to mention my husband, and I'm not quite ready for him to "go."

Thank you, officer, for being so nice; your mother and father sure did a good job raising you. You have a good evening now, ya hear? Be sure to tell my nephew hello for me.

Heading home and a bit miffed by the officer's reactions, I am thinking. . .

What an experience. That officer looked at my driver's license, and then he looked at me. He looked at me sort of like the doctor did when I said that I had only graduated from high school a few years ago. I'll bet the officer would have given me a ticket if he had thought I was an *old* and careless driver. Imagine that. That's something good to know when I do get *old*. I need to be real careful when I am driving and watch out for all the crazy things that can happen.

• • • • • • •

Was this a true story? No, not really, but as we age, anything is possible. Do I wear hearing aids? No, but if I ever do, you can count on me to keep them turned up so I can hear the horns blowing, even if I am the culprit that caused the horns to blow. It is a puzzle to me, the number of people who wear hearing aids and don't keep them turned on or up so that they can hear what is being said to them. They are constantly asking you what you have said. I just don't understand the theory behind it—having something useful and not using it to its full service.

Do I have a nephew that is an officer with the Mount Airy Police Department? Yes, as a matter-of-fact I do, but even before he was on the police force, I always admired and respected the young men and women that serve to protect each one of us. Their job is stressful, and as thankless as the teachers', and on a daily basis they have to deal with sometimes life-threatening situations, and even situations much like the little old lady in the story. Most of the time, the officers are kind, courteous, and tolerant; but we should always remember that, if someone is expected to be nice, let it be me or you; why shouldn't we set the example?

So, if ever you are stopped by a police officer, keep your cool. He or she is doing a job that your taxes pay for. Your safety is in his or her hands. Take seriously the situation you are in at the time and show respect. So what if someone sees the blue light behind your car or mine? So what if we are given a ticket? Life goes on. We'll live through it. And, most of all, if we receive a ticket, it is most likely that we deserved it.

● ● ● ● ● ● ●

Now, I am pondering the good daughter-in-law, or you might say, the too young to understand daughter-in-law...

Oh my, how we remember strange things as we get a little older. I remember the many Sundays that I would sit in church between my mother-in-law and Claude. I can remember how stone still she could sit the entire service and how I somehow managed to put on *"undies"* every Sunday with wiggle beans, because I constantly felt the need to move something—cross my legs; fold my arms; turn a little; turn a little the opposite way; take a deep breath; scratch my nose; scratch my arm. I was like the little child that had a *"can't-sit-still-syndrome."* How in the world did she manage to sit for forty-five minutes without moving? One day, I got up the nerve and asked, "Mom, how can you sit so still and not move in church?"

With that question, I fell into a deep mud pit, face first. She firmly looked me straight in the eyes; without any facial changes and said, "Shirley, I consider it very rude and annoying to those around me if I am moving. It is very possible that I would be disturbing someone."

Oops, I thought. Wonder how many times I have bothered and annoyed her with my squirming?   I knew I would have to come up with another way to please her and stay in her good favor because I remember wondering each Sunday after that—how in the world can I possibly sit still another minute, and another minute, and another minute, and another?

It's difficult to know if I ever got anything out of the sermon on those Sundays, but there was one good thing; when the pastor repeated a sermon sometime later—and some pastors do, you know—we tend to capture that which went right past us the first time around.

● ● ● ● ● ● ●

I had a wonderful mother-in-law, but I was always trying to prove to her that I loved her son and that I was the right one for him. A few years before her death, I finally realized that she had accepted me and probably had accepted me much sooner than I had ever conceived.

Isn't it funny, how we allow our thoughts and crazy ideas to influence ridiculous (and probably inaccurate) assumptions?

So many times, a young daughter-in-law and a new mother-in-law just don't give each other a chance. Too many times, the breakup of a friendship—or the lack of molding a strong friendship between the two—is caused by selfish and controlling personalities of one or both of them, but, isn't this true of all types of relationships?

Don't forget, mothers; the children are only **loaned** *to us; they* **are not** *our possessions. When he or she marries, let that child be* *the husband to his wife and the wife to her husband, the way God planned.* **Cut the apron-strings.**

Mothers of daughters, let her go. Encourage her to love and to support her new spouse. Encourage her to **not** *run home or call each time there is a disagreement.* **Cut the apron-strings**.

Mothers, stay out of your child's marriage. Your child's marriage is a three-some, and that does not mean you; that means God and the two of them.

Ouch; that hurt someone. Sorry, but you don't want to be the reason if the marriage folds. It has a better chance of surviving and being stronger if God is their source of direction and not me or you.

• • • • • • •

Many years ago, I made up my mind that, when I got older, I would not let the following happen to me. I would know how to avoid it . . . yeah, right! The mind of the "young blood" strikes again . . .

I remember the many Sundays, sitting in church, behind the older ladies—the gray-haired ladies. I remember deciding that . . . when I get their age, I will have trained my hair to do as it is directed to do. My hair won't have that look—the look that I forgot to comb the back section of my head. No sir, . . . not my hair!

Now look at me . . . I have become one of them . . . Must be in the "*jeans.*" Those "*jeans*" are the down-fall of me.

My hair has control of me as if it were a new child that I have been given to raise. My hair knows what it wants to do and does it, no matter how hard I try to train it to do something else . . . Stubborn . . . Without direction . . . Wild and unruly . . . just like a new child and some older children I've known pretty well.

I'll show you, you misfit of a child that covers the head . . . I'll wear a hat on Sundays; that way, only I and God will know what lurks under the brim and the controlling, ungodly actions of this hair of mine.

I must say that I feel a bit of guilt each time someone says that they like my hat. They are being kind and very honest—which I appreciate—but over my head is the lie to my hair, concealing the truth—the lie of the hat-head women. When the hat comes off, out comes the wrath of the hair and its determination to rule.

• • • • • • •

Isn't it interesting how vain we can be? We allow our appearance to become our domineering thought, and, many times this is reflected in our actions.

There is nothing wrong in taking pride in ourselves, but if we allow our looks to control us, they have become an obsession. That which controls us is the sinful nature within us. Look out, honey— no preaching allowed here.

I want to be in control, and if I allow something other than myself to determine my actions, then I am no longer in control. That which controls me has become the god of my life. So, am I allowing my hair to control my actions on Sunday? No, not really. I actually like wearing hats and began wearing them long before I got the "hair with its own mind" problem.

How can we serve God, and see him more clearly, and feel his presence so completely, if we are consumed with ourselves?

If God is in control of me, there is not enough room for me, my controlling hair, and God. Okay, Lord, let it be just you and me—a two-some.

• • • • • • •

I have always had a tendency to be overweight. I am the yo-yo that you hear about; I'm constantly on a string, moving in and out, never knowing if I'll ever be the "Yo-o" in yo-yo. The "Yo-o"—look at me—when I am at the ideal weight, as I was in my 20's (like Miss America) and now, as I should be in my 60's, according to the health charts.

I've always said that God has 'allowed' me to be overweight—not obsessive; we all know that is unhealthy—but I'm just enough overweight so that I won't want to "flaunt" my body. I might have gone the way of the women in a 'house of ill-repute.' God would really have had to deal with me, even more than He does now.

Seriously, be conscious of your appearance; that is important—but allow your appearance to glorify our Father in Heaven. Outwardly, we should be what our heart reveals—genuine in "The Spirit"—the Spirit of the Holy Father.

Don't let your day be ruined because the hair is out of place—put on a hat. It will soon become obvious to everyone that you may be having a bad-hair-day. God loves you, and so do others . . . in spite of your hair and for that matter, in spite of all the other idiosyncrasies.

Chapter 10

Reflections . . . So many changes . . . yet . . .

Gosh, how so much has changed since I was a child at home, and interestingly, as time has passed, some things are still the same, some things—except my age. I'm "60." When was I a child? When did I age? When did I become 60-years-old? . . . I can't be "60" . . . and yet . . . I remember . . .

I remember . . . the summers—always on a Sunday—so many years ago, and yet . . . seems like only a few years ago that I could hear mother say, "I sure would like some ice cream." That could only mean one thing—*homemade ice cream.*

I remember . . . mother would call a taxi—we couldn't afford a car. Mother would have the driver take us to the City Ice Plant, where we would buy ice and rock salt. The ice always had to be just the right size or, as Mother would say, "The ice cream won't freeze the way it should." *(I don't know if there is anything to that, but if Mother believed that, it was okay by me. She was the one with the recipe, and she always made the best ice cream)*

The thrill of what was to come still augments my thoughts. Mercy me . . . how I remember turning the crank on the old ice cream maker until my arm would ache with pain. Mother and I would take turns turning the handle and waiting . . . turning the handle and waiting . . . turning the handle and waiting; it seemed like forever for the ice cream to harden.

Waiting for the ice cream to harden reminds me of taking trips with a young child and hearing him or her constantly ask, "Are we there yet?" *There is no way of knowing the number of times I must have asked,* "Is the ice cream ready yet?"

I remember that, finally, when the handle would not turn one more time, I would ask if we could have some ice cream right then, knowing all along Mother's answer. "Not just yet, honey; we need to let it set for a few minutes more so it will get a little harder." By then, I was ready to drink the ice cream because runny or hard, I knew it would still taste so good.

Mother knew just how to make the ice cream perfect to the taste and firm enough to look almost like store-bought ice cream. I remember how we would eat and eat, bowl after bowl, until our stomachs were so full they hurt.

Has it been that long since we were sitting on the front steps .. . on those hot summer days . . . making and enjoying all we could of Mother's wonderful homemade ice cream? How long ago was that? Am I really *"60?"* How can this be? When did this happen to me? It hasn't been that long since I graduated from high school . . . has it?

• • • • • •

Homemade ice cream we made with our children never—to me—came out quite as good as my mother's, but perhaps they can still remember the few times we did make ice cream. Our children were never able to enjoy the "pain" of hand cranking. Somehow, the manual turning of the handle made me appreciate the ice cream a little more as a child than I did with the electric ice cream maker that we used with our children.

Can you remember the old-time, "hand-crank," ice cream machine, and the old wooden container that held the cylinder, that held the liquid? What are your memories? Take a little time to think about times from the past. Has much changed since you were a child? Is ice cream as good now as it was then? Some companies have ice cream they call 'Homemade', but it sure does miss the mark of the homemade ice cream that I remember. I guess their recipe is a modern form of homemade. Being more modern does make a difference, don't you think?

Who really takes the time these days—or makes the time—to go through the process involved with making homemade ice cream? Many a home has the modern, electric, ice cream maker sitting in storage. The owners—no doubt—decided that "it was too much trouble," once they had purchased it and used it a few times.

• • • • • • •

For some . . . much has changed in what seems like such a short period of time . . .

I remember . . . not so long ago . . . my graduating class was the last graduating class that was not integrated. How can this be? Why did it take so long for such an important change?

I can remember riding the city bus with my mother, so many times, and wondering, so many times, why I **had to** sit in the front of the bus. I always thought the black people had the best seats. They got to sit in the very back of the bus. I thought they were so lucky.

Also, I remember people calling them by another name, but I always called them black people, because—even as a child—somehow within my child's mind, I didn't like the sound of the word that so many people used when speaking of black people. I didn't like to be called names, and I always thought black people were being called names each time I heard this particular word.

When integration became law, I remember thinking, "Great! Now I can sit in the back of the bus and no one can say a thing to me." I thought it was so neat the first time I got to go to the back of the bus and how neat it was that everyone sat wherever they wanted to. Some of the black people still sat in the back, and some of the white people kept sitting in the front, but I got to sit right where I had always thought was the best seat of all—the very back.

• • • • • •

Oh . . . the mind of a child. If we adults don't influence a child to pick the colors of M & M's he or she can eat, why should we be so determined to brainwash a child to think that the color of the skin determines the quality of the person? Each one of us got here the same way—through conception, and each one of us will leave the same way—we'll stop breathing.

Lifestyles and circumstances throughout our lives are different, but the love we should have for one another should mirror that of Christ Jesus.

This thought reminds me of something that happened a few months ago. I went back to school when I was 57-years-old, in pursuit of a degree that I felt strongly God was leading me to earn. After I had taken all the prerequisites required for the degree and had entered into the program—

just prior to turning 60-years-old—I realized, now more than ever, that God was using me to be the shoulder for the younger students, not necessarily for me to earn the degree I was working toward.

There was constant stress placed on each student; therefore, I often observed lashing out of students toward one another. At one point, I was the one being lashed out at, but with God's wonderful way of dealing with every situation we have, it did not affect me the way it did the one that was doing the lashing.

Later in the evening, I received a phone call from that young lady, apologizing to me for her actions. God was so wonderful, and I am so grateful that he allowed me the wisdom to respond in a loving and honest way.

I remember saying, "Honey, don't worry about what happened today. I understand the pressure we are all under. I think you are a precious and a sweet girl to take the time to call me. I don't want you to worry any more about what happened today and just remember that I love you."

She said to me, "Shirley, no one has ever said that I was precious before. I've been called much worse things, but certainly not precious or sweet."

The next day after a test, as students were waiting in the hall until everyone had completed the test, this same young girl came and stood by me. As we talked and laughed, others came up.

Somewhere in the conversation, she said to those around us, "Shirley says that she thinks that I am precious and sweet."

With that, I responded (calling her name), "_____, I certainly do think you are precious, and do you know why? I look at you through the same eyes that God sees you. I look at you through

Christ's eyes. He sees you as his precious child, so how can I not see you the same way, too?"

I still love that precious young lady and each of my special class-mates. Some of them used words that they knew I was offended by—not Christ honoring words—and, bless their hearts, they worked hard not to use them around me.

It is a good practice to look at others through the eyes of Christ. It is amazing what we are blind to and what we really see. The eyes of Christ have blinders on them, and we would serve Christ well to wear blinders more freely.

• • • • • • •

Sixty-years-old . . . Hard to believe . . . So much has changed, and yet, so little, too. Have you taken a look at the color of young people's hair these days, the length of the guys' hair, the style of the shoes, the lengths of the dresses, the many punc-tures to the body (piercing), and, unfortunately, the puncture marks from needles?

*Some things haven't changed that much since you and I were young . . . have they?   The only changes are that there are more of the same things being done today as there was 60-years-ago; more people are getting more pierces in more locations on the body. Peer pressure continues to take over the minds of the young as well as the old, creating a desire to "**not be different**" and, in some cases, a desire to not be alike—to make a statement.*

The dresses are way up or way down in length; the shoes are spiked or squared; the tattoos are not just on the sailors anymore and not just in one or two places, and they now come in colors. Jewelry designers have created jewelry for the nose, the brows, the ears, the toes, the tongue, the thumbs, the belly and I dare to mention other possible places. No longer do we see the ring finger as the only part of the hand flashing a stone, a pearl, or a band.

● ● ● ● ● ● ●

Our home wasn't exempt from the fads of the times . . .

I remember . . . seems just a few years ago, that my boys were still at home, playing football, riding go-carts, playing the guitar.

I remember one year when Claude and I had taken a business trip to California. A day or two after we had arrived home, I had Frank help me clean his bathroom. As we were cleaning it, I glanced at Frank in the mirror, and to my shocked eyes, I saw an earring in one of his ears. As close as I can remember the conversation, this is the way it went . . .

"Frank, what is that in your ear?"

"It's an earring, Mom."

"When did you have that done?"

"Oh, before you left for California."

"Frank, you didn't have that when we left. I don't remember ever seeing it before."

"Mama, it hasn't been there long, really. Are you mad because I got my ear pierced? Do you think Daddy will be upset?"

I took Frank by the hand and lead him to the family room where one wall had pictures of each of the children, and I pointed to them and said,

"Frank, take a look at those pictures. God gave me three children—two boys and one girl—and ***you are not that girl***!"

Frank looked at me with eyes that filled with disappointment in himself for thinking that he had let us down, knowing that was not quite what we expected of him. He asked again if I thought Dad would be upset.

Well, when Claude came in from work, Frank approached him with the new ear ornament. Needless to say, Claude was as shocked as I was. Frank proceeded to find out what Claude's thoughts were.

"Dad, are you upset that I got my ear pierced?"

"Frank, I'm not upset, but I am a bit shocked and disappointed."

"Dad, you're not mad at me, are you?"

"Well, Frank, let me put it this way; when all the family is out at a restaurant, Mother and I will sit at a separate table; and when we all go somewhere, I will drive my car, and you can ride in a separate car; and when we go to church, you can sit a few pews away."

Keep in mind that Claude was saying all this with a chuckle in his voice and a smile on his face, but Frank, in his wisdom, never wore the earring in our presence. Our family still ate and worshipped together as a family. Frank, by his own choice, only wore the earring when he was with his buddies.

David may have had a pierced ear, too, but I don't remember it if he did. He never revealed his secret if there was an earring under his hair. David had the most beautiful long— slightly wavy—shoulder-length hair. (The interesting thing about David is that he now keeps his head completely shaved. His oldest daughter, Hayley, has seen pictures of him when he was in high school with long hair, and she says she likes him better with no hair. It is all about what we are familiar with, I suppose)

Claude and I always said there were worse things our boys could be doing than growing long hair and wearing an earring. We could accept these fads with no problem, if we had a choice between all the other fads and the two our boys had chosen.

● ● ● ● ● ● ●

Never, never, never form the opinion that a child's adult

life is determined by where they come from or by what they are allowed or not allowed to do when they are children. The worst situations can mold and develop the most respected and loved adult, just as the best situation that a child can grow up in doesn't determine the quality of the adult that he or she will become.

Long hair; clown red, pink, and yellow matted hair; tattoos that cover the body; or piercing in places that holes were not made by God; or being on a high from drugs or alcohol doesn't mean these people are hopeless—for the moment they may be helpless, but not hopeless.

God's eyes haven't closed, and he hasn't moved or let go of them. They may be unsightly, and not easy to love—much less tolerate—but they were made by the same hands and love that the straight-laced fellow was made with. Prayer is heard. Faith is not always seeing in order to understand.

Parents . . . don't give up. Don't quit. Love unconditionally. You don't have to like or understand what your child or children do, but keep that love strong, without boundaries. God is listening and responding.

I've walked or am walking down some of the same paths you are now walking or have walked, and I know that "waiting" to see changes is a hard daily task.

I recently made up my mind . . . no more arguing or fussing, and I relayed this message to several people that I have had the most discord with.

My words were, "There has been enough fussing and arguing between us to last a lifetime. I want to have peace and calm until I die, and I want this for others, as well."

Nothing is gained, but much is lost, each time there is discord between a parent and child, a friend and a friend, a spouse and a spouse. Look at each situation where there was discord between you and the other person. Who gained anything from it? How much was lost because of it?

Why couldn't I have been much wiser, much sooner? More sleep would have been gained, and there would have been much less worry and fewer tears. I am still saying, "Let it go, Shirley; God can stay up all night. All I have to do is pray and believe. He takes care of all the rest."

Chapter 11

Reflections . . . From friends . . .
To trips . . . To Donald Trump

Friendships . . . thank goodness for memories that include special friends. I just finished talking with Evelyn—my third-place best friend. (She's trailing God in first place and Claude in second place. That's not a bad position to be in)

Gosh, we've been friends for thirty-five years . . . but how can that be? Today, I feel as though I should be only 22 or 23. Where has time gone? What has happened in-between?

We're now planning a trip for the fall, but we'll just have to wait and see. Reservations are made, and dates to leave are scheduled . . . but things can change . . . we'll wait and see.

We know that the plans we make are subject to change by the time we wake up each day—we have learned to adjust . . . to accept the things we can't change . . .

That sure is not the way I thought forty or fifty years ago. I wanted everything now … can't wait … now, now, now; just like the youth of today—give me instant mashed-potatoes and a microwave meal. And if I make plans, nothing better change them!

Rayburn, Evelyn, Claude, and I have taken many trips together—since 1995, when Claude retired—so many memorable trips. We've experienced and shared some really funny and fun trips, as well as some strange and unusual trips.

Gosh, seems like just a few years ago . . . actually, it was only a few months before Claude retired that Evelyn and I traveled to Germany—our first trip together—to visit with David, Tara, and Hayley. Sheldon had not been born yet. The children were living in Orsfeld, a small village that is 9 kilometers—about 5.6 miles—Northeast of Bitburg and 56.33 kilometers—about 35 miles— from Trier (*a wonderful historical town with roman baths and winding streets*). There were no extra bedrooms in their barn-converted-apartment, much less beds, so Evelyn and I shared the couch-to-bed sleeping area.

This was around the time that same-sex relationships were becoming more widely known, and Evelyn and I had no intentions of anyone ever getting the idea that we were of *that* group. When bedtime came, Evelyn said, "That is your side, and this is my side." There was an imaginary line running down the middle of our couch-bed, and we silently understood that it was not to be crossed by either of us.

A night or two later and sometime during the night, I woke myself by jerking a foot away from Evelyn when it had accidentally touched her leg. I lay there in the dark, hoping that I had not awakened her—then she moved.

In silence and pitch black, Evelyn started laughing and said in a loud whisper, "You touched me, didn't you?" I replied, also in a loud whisper, "I didn't mean to. I was hoping I hadn't awakened you and that you were still asleep." She said, "I was asleep until you touched me." Needless-to-say, that was the ice-breaker. She and I laughed at that strained sleeping arrangement the rest of the trip; we even get a good laugh out of it to this day.

The innocence of our friendship had been strained by our own fears and by allowing social lifestyles to determine our comfort level with our friendship.

Real friendships don't require us to see or talk with one another each and every day. Friendships have no barriers and no time frame. Friendships understand each other's feelings, carry each others sorrows, listen when we need to talk, and speak when we need to hear the truth. A friend is our sister or our brother when we have none— our family when we are left alone.

The trip Evelyn and I took to Germany was the beginning of our travels together. After we returned from Germany and the four of us were talking about Claude's retirement, I said to Rayburn, "Rayburn, when Claude retires, we are leaving for Alaska, and we would like for you and Evelyn to join us, but if you go, you and Evelyn will have to buy your own motorhome. Our motorhome sleeps six, but it is only big enough for Claude and me." *(They did, and that was the beginning)* ● ● ● ● ● ● ●

Wow . . . 60-years-old . . . Sure doesn't seem as though I should be here yet . . . and yet . . . how could I have experienced so many things if I were younger? I'm certainly not ready to be "60" because I know what follows— eventually . . . and yet, . . . here I am, "60." How can this be? When did this really happen to me?

Is this what "60" is all about? It's looking back . . . sometimes with tears . . . sometimes with joy, seeing, remembering, feeling some of the same emotions I had way back . . . as if I never left

. . . as if I am still there—there right now—reliving some of my childhood . . . reliving and hearing the words that hurt . . . learning very young the ugliness within some of those I lived near . . .

I remember . . . seems like not so long ago, when I was a child and was walking to a friend's house to play . . . As I walked to her house, I was thinking . . .

K's mother and father are different from the rest of the neighbors. They are always kind to me and treat me so special. I like to play at K's, and K is my best friend. (*I realized years later why her parents were so different. They practiced living as Christ would live*)

Once I got to K's, she suggested that we go next door to play with another neighbor girl. I remember walking home a short time later and thinking about what had just happened and wondering why . . .

As we began to play in K's next-door-neighbors' basement with their daughter, the girl said to me, "Shirley, you will have to go home." "Why?" I asked, and she said, "Because my parents don't want me to play with you." Again, I asked why. She responded with, "Because they are afraid of what you might teach me."

I remember leaving, as I was told to, and crying as I walked home and wondering—what could I teach her? I don't understand what she means. What in the world could I teach her that she didn't already know? What exactly did her parents mean?

I never went back to my friend's house after that, because she might want us to play with the girl next door, and I knew that I wasn't allowed there. I guess this was the time in my life that I finally realized that I was different—not in a physical way, but because of my home life.

I remember thinking for a long time after that . . . what could I teach the neighbor girl? I wondered if maybe the reason I wasn't allowed to play there was because mother worked as a waitress in truck-stops and was a bar maid—in order to make enough money to pay the bills. Was it because Mother and Daddy were divorced?

I just couldn't understand what a difference that would make. I knew mother had no choice of jobs, because she had only a third-grade education, and I knew that I was the only child in the neighborhood in a divorced family, but I kept thinking … what is it that I am supposed to know that I can teach to another child?

I kept thinking . . . For goodness sakes, Mother is a kind and hard-working woman. She smokes, and all she drinks is coffee. She has high morals and teaches me to be a good person. She hasn't dated anyone since Daddy left, and no men ever come to the house. I have never once seen Mother kiss a man or show any fondness toward a man . . .

I decided that I would never tell Mother about what had happened and what I was told. As young as I was, I knew Mother would be hurt.

Interesting, how so much has changed since way back then and how painful that situation was. I never saw my friend "K" again, until a number of years later when my mother died. My friend worked in the oncology department of the hospital Mother was in. Mother's name caught her eye as she was filling an order for platelets for Mother and, by God's hands, we met again. Mother later died, and my friend went on to live in another state.

The neighbor's daughter became a "Breck" Hair Spray Model with her face and beautiful hair seen on the hair spray cans. The last I heard about her was that she continued to be a model in New York and frequented dinner parties that were given by the well-known "Donald Trump." I wonder if she could now teach me a few things that I've never heard or thought about.

Interesting, how our lives make so many different turns from birth, through childhood, then adulthood. We can let the painful parts of our lives eat us alive or we can learn and grow from those painful situations.

• • • • • • •

Please take a moment and reconnect with your years gone by. Were there moments when you were a child that you just can't shake off? A time when you were hurt by an adult or another child's words or actions? It's time to forgive them; even if you can't go to them, do it in your heart.

Were you the adult or the child that painfully crushed another child with your words or actions? Perhaps, now is a good time to ask for forgiveness. You or I may not be able to go to that person, but God will listen, respond, forgive, and forget.

We must guard against the piercing words that can come from our mouths. As a child or as an adult, the pain is the same. As the Bible tells us, our tongue is like a two-edged sword; once released—the damage is done, and we can't return the words from whence they came.

Chapter 12

Reflections . . . What has happened at age 20, 30 . . . 40—"Diamonds" and 50

As I try to figure out when I got to the age of "60" so quickly, I begin rethinking of what was happening in my life at age 20, age 30, age 40, and age 50 . . .

I can't be 60-years-old. When did this happen to me? Let me think. OK brain, give me the facts! . . . I was a mother of three by the time I was 25-years-old . . . That is a fact . . . There is no wondering if that really happened. I have the scars, the wrinkles, and the stretch marks to prove it.

I don't know if I have gray hair that came from the three extensions that sprang—well not really sprang—from my body because my bottle-blonde hair doesn't reveal the truth of the covering of my otherwise bald head.

I'm not quite sure what happened to the five years between 25 and 30, but somewhere during that time . . . I *know* something happened . . . I *think*!

I clearly remember turning 30. I didn't mind turning 30, but I remember getting punished for it. I remember . . . I was a short-stop on a ladies slow-pitch softball team, and I remember how ***good*** I was. Oh yeah, that is a fact! I was *good*. I'm not real sure anyone else knew how good I was, but I knew.

The day I turned 30, I thought, no big deal. I went on to the game . . . and . . . I had to sit on the bench the entire game. What a bummer . . . "30" . . . and on the bench. How could this be? Don't these people realize this is my day? I'm 30-years-old—they could at least say "Happy Birthday."

Well . . . I'll show them . . . keeping me on the bench on my birthday . . . I just won't have another 30th birthday for them to ignore. I'll show them . . . and I did show them, because the next birthday I had I was "40."

Absolutely nothing happened in-between. I was 30-years-old one day and the next thing I knew . . . I was "40."

Forty was the one to remember. That was the age I gained respect. It was the strangest thing. Before I was 40-years-old, no matter what I said, no one listened, and I thought that some of the stuff I said was pretty good, too.

Once I turned "40," I began repeating everything that I said before I turned "40," and suddenly . . . I'm the one everyone wants to listen to. I became intelligent in ten years. Maybe that's why I don't remember anything between 30 and 40. I was in a state of *"becoming smart"*; therefore, I don't remember anything. Figure that out.

I remember that, after I turned 30, and no one had recognized my big day, except me and Mother, I remember telling Claude, "When I turn "40," I want you to do something *big* for me." Claude reminded me that he had ten years to worry about that. I know that we women make plans way in advance, and men make plans very close to the deadline of any special event, but I had given him fair warning. *Ten* years is plenty enough time to prepare to not forget.

Six months before I turned 40, I reminded Claude that my birthday was coming up, and I wanted to do something special. He said, "Ok honey, I'm working on it."

Three months before I turned 40, I again reminded Claude that my birthday was coming up, and I wanted to do something special. Again he said, "Ok honey, I'm working on it."

Two weeks before my 40th birthday came, I asked Claude what we were going to do to celebrate my 40th birthday. He said, "I was going to take you to the Grove Park Inn in Asheville for a few days." *Wow, that sounds great, I thought;* then he finished with, "Guess I waited too long to make reservations. They are booked for your birthday week and the weekend before and after. What do you have in mind that we can do now?"

Inside, I was yelling, "**W H A T? . . . You've had ten years to get ready for this day; how can the Grove Park Inn be booked?**"

Disappointed, but not destroyed, yet . . . I said, "How about buying me some diamond studs?" (*I had waited until I was 38-years-old before I took the plunge and became one of those Jezebels that I said I would never become—I got my ears pierced—and now I wanted to go the second mile as a Jezebel and have diamonds. Our daughter, Jackie, had gotten her ears pierced when she was 19-years-old, and I thought they looked really nice, so Frank—our oldest son—gave me the money to have my ears pierced for my 38th birthday gift from him. Wow, I did remember something that happened between the time I was 30-years-old and 40-years-old)*

"Diamonds; you're kidding, of course," were the loving words that came from the mouth of the man of my dreams. *I'm thinking,* "Sugar . . . you blew it ten years ago when you didn't start making plans for this 40th birthday, and you think I'm kidding when I say *diamonds.* Not a skinny chance am I kidding."

Our youngest son David was still living at home and said, "Dad, I think you should buy Mama some diamond earrings; she deserves them."

My 40th birthday came. All day, I waited and waited for "something" from Claude. He sent me a card—that I had to walk to the mail box to get myself. Late that evening, the doorbell rang with a delivery of flowers—the third arrangement I had received that day—and I remember saying to Claude, "If these flowers are not from you, I'm going to cry."

My knight in shining armor replied with, "Well, I guess you'll just have to cry, because they aren't from me."

I'm thinking, what's with this character I married? Has my knight in shining armor been stolen right out of his own body and been replaced with this thoughtless monster?

I thought, no problem, my sweets . . . if the flowers aren't from you, I will cry . . . and cry is exactly what I did, but with every tear, came a plan that shaped the next day's activities. The next day, I took a little drive to Winston-Salem to purchase the *"diamond earrings"* from the man of my dreams . . . but without his knowledge—at least for the time being.

Several, several, weeks passed when, one day, as Claude and I were out enjoying a country drive after breakfast, I asked him, "Would you like to see what you got me for my 40th Birthday?" I remember him asking, "Did I get you something for your 40th Birthday?" As he was looking over at me, I was flipping an ear lobe back and forth with total delight and said, "How do ya like 'um?"

That took care of him remembering me on my birthday for years to come, and now it really doesn't matter to me at all whether a gift is given. I was still too young then to understand the unimportance of being remembered on a birthday. My hormones, or lack thereof, determine a lot about how I respond on my birthdays these days, including the 50th.

Isn't it interesting how we let society—peer pressure—and the way others celebrate a birthday with an "0" in it—determine how we would like to have our big "0's" celebrated?

Turning "50" was another non-eventful day; no black balloons— thank goodness; no black roses—thank goodness; no big celebration with lots of friends—now that would have been nice—lots of friends. Guess I need lots of friends for that kind of party. So life goes on, and on, and on.

Working through Beth Moore's <u>Living Beyond Yourself</u> Bible Study is a study I should have done years ago. Perhaps the old selfish me would have had much happier "0's.'" How important did I think I was, anyway?

How much emphasis do you place on events in your life? Does life go on for you if you are not shown special attention on a special occasion, or do you allow yourself to ruin your own day and the day of others because you expected something that did not develop?

Think back to some of your previous birthdays, Mother's

Days, or anniversaries. Were you anticipating something that did not happen? How did you react? How "important" did you think you were? Have you changed, or do you still simmer until you explode?

We may be disappointed and broken-hearted if we are not remembered, but life goes on, doesn't it? Our reaction to everything determines what will follow. It is up to us, isn't it? We need to be thankful that we have made it to another birthday. What a birthday present we've received. God gave us another year. Shout hurrah! Praise your Father—you made it.

Lord, forgive my selfish, human attitudes . . . for you have given me a super birthday gift—one more year.

● ● ● ● ● ● ●

Ok, I made it to "50." I remember "40." I remember "30." I remember . . . nope . . . I still don't remember "20."

What in the world happened between age "40" and age "50?" Ten years—time that I have been living somewhere in between, and I cannot recall anything happening . . . except . . .

I remember "42." I gave up chocolate, and I remember not eating chocolate for six years. I remember giving up chocolate again at age 50 and not eating it until I was 60-years-old. I must be a real coo-coo. Why would anyone remember something so ridiculous? I must be deprived of something . . . perhaps my brain. I am brain deprived, or could it be that I am Chocolate deprived?

"*><)#^ **"60"** ^#(<>" I must be "^^^**60**^^^" No, I'm not brain deprived . . . I'm **OLD.** I'm there—"60"—but how can this be? I just graduated from high school a few years ago . . . didn't I???????

Ah, "50." Being "50" wasn't so bad. Gosh, the things I did that I never had the opportunity to do—or the guts to do—before I was "50."

Between "50" and "60," my friend, Evelyn, and I confidently, yet fearfully tried tandem para-sailing—over the Florida Keys—while our brave husbands looked on with shock and disbelief. Of course, by this time in my life, my bladder was deplorably over-active. Thank goodness we were lowered into the water before we were finally pulled back into the boat; otherwise, everyone in the boat would have known that I had *wet my pants*.

Between "50" and "60," Evelyn and I Glacier River Rafted on class four rapids near Denali in Alaska, while our brave husbands took pictures from the dry, dry land.

Between "50" and "60," Claude and I enjoyed snowmobiling at Yellowstone National Park—for several years—before snowmobilers were required to have a guide.

The "50's" were wonderful—half-a-century, half-a-hundred. At what age does a person become an antique? Is it "50?" If that is the case, I am at last worth something, but, then worth what, to whom, and how little change would someone be willing to forfeit? Who would buy an old worn out granny of an antique that is rusty, squeaky, non-repairable, wrinkled, dented, living without all her bodily parts and in bad need of a new paint job?

It's certainly something to think about. Claude did say that I could be replaced. Now is not the time to figure out how quickly that statement could take real meaning. This is scary. Yep. Some sweet young thing with all her body parts and a new paint job could come along and . . . and . . . I'd scare the breath right out of her. I may be *old*, and I may be "50," and a possible antique, but I'm not dead. Look out, honey. You're tangling with a mean, "50" fighting machine.

Chapter 13

Reflection . . . Facing the facts—I am "60"

Well, here I am . . . 60-years-old. I absolutely do not understand how or when I got to this time in my life. It seems like only a few years ago since I graduated from high school, but I know that just can't be possible.

The trees outside the doors are no longer skinny. The children are no longer in diapers. We now live on a fixed income—more fixed than when the children were in elementary school, high school, and college.

My hair is thinner and just as straight as it always was, but the skin just isn't the same. I'm shorter and rounder and on pills for high blood pressure and cholesterol. I move slower than I'd like to . . .

So, where do I go from here? All these thoughts inaugurate more thoughts . . .

I remember Claude saying to me early in our marriage, "Grow old along with me; the best is yet to be." Growing together has been great, but the growing old is not what it is framed to be by the picture the world around us paints . . .

As I read articles, with celebrities talking about how wonderful it is to be "50" and "60," I think, "Honey if I had the dollars that it takes to have a personal trainer, a personal chef, my own personal diet expert, a personal housekeeper, a lawn maintenance man, someone to walk the dog and clean the cat litter boxes, then perhaps being "60" would be grand."

In all the articles I have read, I have never heard anyone say, I am so excited to be "50," come on "60," I can't wait to be "70," . . . and "80" will be wonderful. Once we pass the "40" mark, and we look at life a little realistically, we know that time is passing by swiftly. We begin to see our parents aging, grandparents become frail, and deep in our not-wanting-to-admit-it minds, we see what we may be like some day.

We exercise, we walk, we run, we stay busy trying not to get old. Maybe we can avoid the aging process. We can beat it. The *it-won't-happen-to-me* syndrome begins to take over. I'll eat right, stay out of the sun, not smoke—that won't be a problem, since I never took up that habit—just drink a glass of wine once in a while—perhaps only at communion—and watch my weight. We do all the "*right*" things, and *we still age*. It happens.

I don't mind being "60", but I do mind all of the luggage that I carry with being "60." Everything I eat turns to something, and usually that something causes something else, which causes something that has to be treated with exercise, medications, a different diet or a new way of living. Anyone who thinks getting old is *grand* hasn't experienced the "old" yet.

People say, "You're only as old as you feel." Bologna. How is that possible? I am as old as I am. Period! How do I know how it feels to be "70" if I've never been "70?" I remember different ages, and how I think I felt at those ages, and at times I'd like to think that I can still do some of the things that I did at those ages, but I'm afraid that if I tried to be as old or as young as I think I feel at the time, I could hurt myself really badly.

Getting old is not always what it is cracked up to be. There is no fun watching your spouse begin to have health problems. There is no joy in being left alone because a spouse of many years has died. Rudeness and disrespect rather than kindness jumps ahead of you in the grocery store, on the highway, or in the malls.

Being "*old*" is no picnic. Strokes happen sometimes, no matter how careful we are with our diet and lifestyle. Being disabled—handicapped—takes away independence that in turn takes away our dignity. Sometimes I'd like to scream, "BE GENTLE WITH ME—I'M NOT DEAD YET—I'M JUST OLD."

Getting old is scary. When we are young, we never see ourselves as old people. That only happened to our grandparents or someone else. I don't mind getting old, but I don't like what could happen as I age. What quality of life will I have?

Will the children become too busy to call or to visit? Will my eyes stay healthy enough to enjoy reading, sewing and doing all the things that my eyes are used for?

Aging . . . it happens. I wasn't ready for it when I was 40, and I'm not ready for it now. But here it is, and so am I . . . aged.

Someone needs to be arrested for defrauding the human race with rumors such as, "Aging is like a good wine," and "We get better with age." Spreading rumors is not nice. What part of the "*We*" gets better? Everything about me is less—not better—than when I was young, except my weight, and it is more—not better. *Ok, Granny, it's time to remember what your mother taught you, "Believe only half of what you see and none of what you hear."*

How good can a good wine—aging—be when it would taste better if you were to spit it out? Spit out the old age and drink in youth. I feel like the unleashed fermentation of the fruit that was in the bottle when the cork was removed. I feel squashed by the pressing of the feet of the ladies in an "old" I Love Lucy Show.

Oh yeah; I'm like "A good wine" ... right. I'm beginning to look like the grapes that have not been picked and were left to shrivel and wrinkle in the heat of the sun. The appearance is the facial expression one reveals when he or she begins to smell unwanted grapes being mixed with hot rotting cabbage. Put the cork back in the bottle, baby, so this *good wine* can age some more. At other times, this *good wine* looks like a "Devil's Spit Cup"—swelled and puffy and ready to explode.

Sixty isn't old ...

Sixty is mature! ...

Sixty isn't old. Compared to what? Sixty isn't old compared to "70." Sixty is old compared to "50," or "40," or "20." I'm old, and I want someone to explain to me when this happened. It hasn't been long since I graduated from high school.

Oh, I know, I'm only mature. Mature ... Honey, do you know what mature means? It means that at "60" I'm at my ripeness. I'm a mature ... "old" ... ripe female who is on my way to decay. Perhaps what I thought were wrinkles are really cobwebs.

This is not quite what I thought being "60" would be like. Actually, I never gave a thought to being "60" until now, and now that I am "60," if I don't start thinking about what it will be like to be "60," I will be "61."

How can this be? I graduated from high school, and only a few years later, I am 60-years-old, and before I realize it, I will be "61."

Hello ... Stop the train. I'm moving entirely too fast, and, at my age, I'll finish the ride before I'm ready. There is still so much I want to do before the ride comes to an end ... but the train is just moving too fast.

Chapter 14

Reflections . . . Accepting being "60" . . . Ready to move on, but slower

Finally, it is beginning to hit me . . . and at times, hard. I am "60," but I just can't understand how this happened so quickly. It seems such a short time ago that I graduated from high school and not so long ago that I was much, much younger.

I recently spent the day with a very special cousin, and I finally felt reality begin to take form as the following picture began to un-fold . . . and then, a change of attitude.

Today, Dianne's family is giving her a surprise "60th" Birthday Bash. Dianne and I have been close friends as well as insepara-ble first cousins (*there were 32 first cousins on our mother's side of the family*) for 60 years, but keep in mind that I had to wait nine months for her to be born before we could begin our adventures. If you follow me, I was born first; therefore, *I am the oldest.*

There was a long time in our teens that Dianne detested me being the oldest because she wanted that *beloved* position. Imagine that! But as years passed, and with each birthday, Dianne would remind me with the same question, "Shirley, guess who's the *youngest*?" She didn't mind me being the oldest, now. We always joked about this *great* age difference, and she would ask me at each birthday, "How does it feel to be the oldest? You are, you know!"

Today was different. We spent a big part of the day together, for the first time since we were teens. Before today, we had never really discussed how old we were, except with a joking comment. We began our outing with a birthday lunch at the comfortable and relaxing Firebirds Rocky Mountain Grill Restaurant—in the new architecturally designed North Hills Shopping Center in Raleigh. As baby boomer music played in the background, and as I was finishing a wonderful entrée of Pecan Crusted Trout and Dianne completed grazing on a Sesame Chicken Salad, she asked *the* pointed question, "Shirley, did you think you would ever be *old*?"

"Old . . . I knew that one day I would be old, but I didn't think it would be so soon," I told her. We both agreed that it doesn't seem like we should be 60-years-old. We can still remember, as if it were yesterday, the things we did when we were teens. It seems like only a few years ago, just a few years, when Dianne and I were in our teens and just a few years since I graduated from high school.

Tempus fugit . . . time really does fly. Just think; in only three months, I will be "61." When I started this book, I was having a difficult time believing that I was "60," and now, I will probably be at least "61" before the book is published. *Tempus fugit.*

When I was younger, I would think about "one day" . . . "One day, when the children are older I will do this or that, or visit aunt . . . or uncle . . . "One day when . . ." I have lived past "one day when." Did I get the chance or take the time to follow through with those ideas? How many aunts and uncles have died that I never got the chance to visit but for only a few times? Where are all my cousins today? Where are their children? How many times are my cousins grandparents? How many are still living, and which ones have died?

Time . . . not a lot of time is left.

M·o·r·b·i·d thoughts . . . quit that, "old" girl. You still have lots of life left in you.

"Sixty" . . . "65" . . . "70" . . . life goes on. There are a few things that can be said about being "60." It is 10 years past "50" and 10 years before "70", and other than that, being 60-years-old is not so bad . . . really.

At "60," I can go and come when I get ready. I can cook or not cook; do the laundry or wait another day; sew; read; write; or paint. My time and how it is used is up to me. I can sleep late or get up early. There are no restrictions, other than the ones I place on myself. I am able to be spontaneous.

Spending hours on the screened in porch, or watching the birds and squirrels feeding on seeds, or enjoying a cool afternoon bath is a daily pleasure at "60," but only a brief luxury for the young.

I can let the wrinkles bother me or give thanks that I still have skin for the wrinkles to find a home to crevice in. I can still dream about places I'd like to visit, and because I am "60," those places I visit can become memories for the time I am "61" . . . . or "62" . . . . or . . .

Living in small town Mount Airy, in the United States, in the year 2006, isn't such a bad time or a bad place to be "60." Life still has so much to offer. My goodness . . . so many books not yet read; people I've not yet gotten to know; adventures that I have yet to experience. Many "roses" not yet enjoyed.

Oh yes, I am mature . . . a relic from the past . . . time-worn, but not crumbling. There is still a lot of life left in this "old" 60-year-old. I'm not yet a fossil and far beyond being a bloom . . . my bones may be decrepit, but they at least still move and perform the directions that my brain gives them.

I'm going through all the stages of aging, just as God planned, but sleeping less and losing some of my taste buds aren't all bad. It's losing my mind that worries me the most, but then, I'll be in good company with a lot of really good friends and family I know.

Sixty . . . how can this be? I'm trying to accept it . . . that "60" is me. But when did this happen? It seems like only a few years ago that I graduated from high school. How can "60" get here so quickly?

Oh well, life goes on. I am "60," soon to be "61."

Help! Help! How can this be? When did this happen to me? I just graduated from high school a few years ago.

• • • • • • •

Big town or small town; house, condo, villa, or apartment; in 2006, or '07, or '08, or earlier, or in the future; it's not such a bad time or place to be the age you are.

Look up . . . look out . . . don't stress on what you see or don't see; what you have or don't have; where you live or wish you could have lived. Stay busy. Enjoy your time to relax, work, and play. Don't dwell on what you cannot do, but do what you are able. No need to worry about what hasn't happened in your life, but be grateful for all that has happened. Take the time to think about all those that are special to you or have been special to you—aunts, uncles, cousins, teachers, special friends, or children. Take the time to visit, write a note, make a call. Take fresh flowers to the grave of a deceased friend or family member. Take the time to pull the weeds from your mind and replace the weeds with sweet peas and sugar plums, joy, peace, and love.

If you are still in your youth, don't wait until another day goes by to visit your parents, family members, or friends. Take them out for the day, and you insist on "footing the bill."

Lean on the older people in your life for words of wisdom. They did not get where they are today without some hurdles to master and their experiences can be of great help for you.

Life is what we make of it at "20" or "60" or at any age. We can become crabby about everything, or we can take each day as it comes and be thankful that we made it one more day.

Be positive about everything. I am positive that I am getting older, good Lord willing, and I am positive that I can still be the best I can be. I am positive that some days aren't as good as others, but I am positive that that may only be temporary, or it may be permanent. I am positive that when I have pain that it hurts. I am positive that the pain can get worse or it can improve. I am positive that God has a plan and that I am included in his plan.

Sixty years . . . only a number . . . and a relatively small number when compared to the number of days in those 60 years. From birth to age 60, we have lived 21,900 days, which makes "60" sound so insignificant. How were those 21,900 days lived? We were learning and growing, stumbling and falling, laughing and crying, alone or among friends, working or relaxing, obedient to Gods guidelines or allowing Satan to guide our lives and our thoughts. These 21,900 days are now past history; nothing can be changed that happened then.

Each day makes a difference . . . the past . . . the present . . . and the future. How will we use the days ahead of us—with a "Baa-Hum-Bug" or a "Hallelujah" attitude? We can still learn and continue to grow. We may still stumble and fall, but we know we can also get up and move on. There continues to be tears, but we must search for smiles among those tears.

Loneliness is difficult, but we are never totally alone. Try setting your table with an extra plate, napkin, and utensils. It's a grand reminder that Christ sits with you.

We're moving forward. Christ holds our hand as we move—by whatever means—into each new day, week, month, and year of our lives.

Happy 60th . . . or 61st, or whatever year you might be . . . The best is yet to be. A lot depends on you and me. We may not be able to blow out all the candles, but we sure can enjoy the cake.

About The Author

Shirley Frances Whittington-Brinkley—an only child of Thomas Nathanial and Helen Hursey Johnson—was born in Conroe, Texas on September 4, 1945 and at an early age moved to Raleigh, North Carolina. She graduated from Needham Broughton High School in 1963 and the same year married State College Graduate, Claude Franklin Brinkley. They moved to Mount Airy, North Carolina (Mayberry), his hometown as well as the hometown of Andy Griffith and Country Western Singer, Donna Fargo.

Claude and Shirley are the parents of a daughter— Jacqueline Dolores and two sons— Claude Franklin (Frank, Jr.) and David Cooke. Claude and Shirley are the grandparents of Christina, Olivia and Baylor, and Hayley and Sheldon. They are also the parents to a special young lady who has made their family complete, their daughter-in-law, Tara Adams Brinkley.

Shirley has traveled from New York to Georgia as a motivational speaker for an International Christian Organization. She does not boast of publishing large numbers of books but takes pride as having published two successful and much loved inspirational cookbooks for her church. The most recent was selected by Oxmoor House, three years in a row, for inclusion in *Hometown Collection* of *America's Best Recipes* and was staff choice for several months at the Moravian Book Store in Old Salem—Winston-Salem, N. C..

She has a broad interest in many activities, which include reading, writing, studying, sewing, traveling and pampering her beloved Claude. She enjoys people, the sound of laughter, and has never met a stranger.

Shirley is passionate about her faith and trust in God. She thrives on serving others and is never too busy to pray, console, guide, talk, and listen when someone needs a caring friend.

Take a look inside and get to know her a little better, for she will strike a chord and hit a few nerves, as you read and enjoy her humorous tales that are woven in with a few heart-touching stories—stories that all women can relate to, regardless of age or position in life.

• • • • • • •

Give the gift of love to Family, Friends, and Colleagues with the book that speaks to women of all ages. A man in your life might also enjoy it and learn just how aging affects "his women." And, for goodness sakes, don't forget you.

Help! Help! When Did This Happen?

I can't be 60-years-old!
I just graduated from high School.

ISBN: 978-0-9676547-1-3

For Fundraisers and to Contact Author:

Shirley W. Brinkley
342 Pineview Drive
Mount Airy, North Carolina 27030-5147
Call: 336.789.1866 or Fax: 336.789.1866
Email: Subject Line: Fundraiser; Book Order; Author
Email: sbbrinkley@earthlink.net

For more books:

1. Check with your bookstore or
2. Catawba Publishing Company – Bookstore
www.catawbapublishing.com

Cost of Book when ordered:

USA $12.75 plus shipping/handling/tax when applicable
Canada $ 12.75 plus shipping/handling
Personal Check or Money Order if ordered from author
Credit Card if ordered from publishing company
Fundraisers: Discuss details with author

*Thank you for your order and allowing me
to be your gift connection*.